Conversations with Fellini

Conversations with Fellini

Edited by

Costanzo Costantini

Translated by Sohrab Sorooshian

A Harvest Original
Harcourt Brace & Company
SAN DIEGO   NEW YORK   LONDON

Requests for permission to make copies of any part of the work should
be mailed to: Permissions Department, Harcourt Brace & Company,
6277 Sea Harbor Drive, Orlando, Florida 32887-6777.

This is a translation of *Conversations avec Federico Fellini*

Library of Congress Cataloging-in-Publication Data
Conversations avec Federico Fellini. English.
Conversations with Fellini/edited by Costanzo Costantini: translated
by Sohrab Sorooshian.—1st U.S. ed.
p. cm.
"A Harvest original."
Previously published: Fellini on Fellini. London:
Faber and Faber, 1995.
Includes index.
ISBN 0-15-600440-2
1. Fellini, Federico—Interviews. 2. Motion picture producers and
directors—Italy—Interviews. I. Costantini, Costanzo.
PN1998.3.F45A5   1996
791.43'0233'092—dc20   96-7959

Text was set in Adobe Garamond.

Printed in the United States of America
First U.S. edition
A B C D E

Contents

Introduction

I first met Federico Fellini in the fifties. I interviewed him for *Il Messaggero,* the Rome daily on the Via del Tritone. The paper's editor at the time was Vincenzo Spasiano, a Neapolitan considered something of a marvel by his colleagues, who stayed in the office until the early hours of the morning, except for the occasional coffee in Settebello, the all-night bar nearby. It was here, in the midst of the kind of human driftwood a Roman night washes up, that I got to know the director from Rimini. We hit it off right from the start. As a former reporter he loved the world of newspaper production and was always delighted to come up to the editorial office, although he preferred to hang around in the printing plant or in the basements where the presses rolled. Thus he became a familiar figure at the paper and from our first meeting I established a close friendship with him.

From the second half of the fifties onward I interviewed Fellini two or more times a year, usually when he was starting a film or when he was finishing shooting. We would meet on the set at Cinecittà or elsewhere: in his office on Via della Croce, Via Sistina or Corso d'Italia; in restaurants; at his Rome address or at his home in Fregene, the seaside resort near Rome where he set his film *The White Sheik.* But we also used to meet on other occasions, which had nothing to do with work.

In April 1975, when he had just learned that he had won an Oscar for *Amarcord*, I called him to request an interview.

"But what do you want me to say? I truly don't know what to say, you must believe me."

"Please, Federico."

"This is the fourth time I've won an Oscar I don't deserve and I can't keep on repeating the same old things."

"All I want is ten minutes, even five."

"Well, come to Via Sistina tomorrow morning at nine, but I tell you again that I have nothing to say."

Just before nine I was at his office.

"I'm sorry you've come all the way here for nothing," he said to me, shaking my hand and embracing me.

There followed a brief silence; then he added, "I really don't know what to say to you."

There followed another brief silence; then he lay down listlessly on the sofa and gestured to me to take a chair beside him.

He talked nonstop until one-thirty.

All at once he remembered that he was late for a lunch appointment. He got up and said, "Excuse me, but I must go. I'm sorry to leave you; I'm in such good spirits when I'm with you. You're one of the few people with whom one can have a proper conversation, an exchange of ideas."

Throughout the time I had spent in his study, I had uttered only one sentence: "Excuse me, I must leave you briefly." Without stirring himself, he indicated with his hand the room I was looking for and on my return resumed his monologue.

He was a fascinating talker. Perhaps only Jorge Luis Borges could reveal, in words, worlds as strange, luminous and seductive. Roberto Rossellini, the only director to whom Fellini would concede the title "maestro," was also an extraordinary interviewee. But the creator of *Rome, Open City* and *Paisà,* both of which Fellini worked on as co-writer and assistant director, would talk not only about his own triumphs and disasters, but also about those of other people;

whereas his "disciple" would talk only about himself, about his own emotional life, about the dazzling imaginary world in which he held absolute sway. "He lies even when he tells the truth," it was said of him. Fellini used to say of himself: "Many people call me a liar, but others are also lying. The greatest falsehoods told about me I have heard from other people. I could have denied them, but since I'm a liar, no one would have believed me." He was a cultivator of untruth, but in the sense given to the word by Oscar Wilde, who considered it a manifestation of the imagination, of inventive talent, of artistic creativity.

The critic Germaine Greer has written that Fellini is the most Italian of filmmakers, if not the most Italian of all Italians. He unites within himself all our contradictions: open and closed, extrovert and introvert, expansive and withdrawn; ambiguous, elusive, slippery: the more one sees of him, the less one knows about him; the more time one spends with him, the less one understands him; the nearer one gets to him, the less one can pin him down. The impressions he would make on one would be constantly changing, like the multiple facets of a prism. Just when one thought one had reached a firm conclusion, everything would be uncertain and unclear again and it was necessary to go right back to square one: a variation on the myth of Sisyphus.

It was always he who directed the course of the interview, even when he appeared distracted or inattentive, depressed or listless, nervy or lost in his own thoughts. He would lead one wherever he wanted to, on mystery tours of unthinkable conversation and astonishing digressions. But he always kept to the outskirts of his being, never allowing one to see the center, the heart of the labyrinth.

From 1990 onward, I became much closer to Fellini, acting as his permanent escort, both official and semiofficial, his "personal reporter." He was the only personality on the international stage toward whom I suspended, so to speak, the exercise of that critical spirit which is indispensable in journalism.

During the second half of October 1990 I accompanied him to Tokyo, where he was to receive the Praemium Imperiale, the Far East's equivalent of the Nobel Prize. "I would have preferred 20 million lire from Canova's to 150 million from Tokyo," he said before our departure, confirming his reluctance to quit Rome (Canova's is the famous Roman café in Piazza del Popolo where he used to meet his friends and acquaintances). This was to be the second longest journey he had ever made, after that to Tulum in Mexico, where he had gone with the plan, subsequently aborted, to make a film based on the stories of Carlos Castaneda. But he tackled it without any great difficulty.

"It's been a kind of odyssey," he said on his arrival at Tokyo, while the news photographers and TV cameramen pestered him and Giulietta Masina, who was always at his side being kind and attentive. But then, after a brief rest, he was in dazzling form. "I'm sorry I wasn't able to prepare a little speech on the plane because the flight was too short," he said in one of the reception rooms of the Okura, the most luxurious hotel in Tokyo, at the start of the press conference that preceded the award ceremony. He then regaled those present with various stories, among them his cherished theory that artists ought to have a patron who should both entice them and threaten them, urging and compelling them to create incessantly, as was the case in Renaissance Italy. "The Praemium Imperiale," he continued, "revives the glorious tradition of the Catholic Church, which understood that the artist is an eternal adolescent and forced him, with enticements and threats, to create immortal masterpieces." Then, in response to journalists' questions, he confessed that he was not familiar with contemporary Japanese cinema, but that he knew well the films of his friend Akiro Kurosawa and cited a sequence from *Rashomon* to demonstrate that the great Japanese director went beyond the bounds of apparent reality in order to grasp at deeper, more spiritual truths, thereby restoring to cinema its former sacred, visionary and mysterious character.

The next day Fellini and Giulietta Masina, in the course of chatting to the people who had gathered in the foyer of the Miyukiza Cinema to watch a screening of *The Voice of the Moon,* engaged in an exhilarating marital-professional skirmish.

"Giulietta is my ideal actress, the one who inspires me, a magic presence in my work," said the director.

"You're lying. I was never allowed to set foot on the set of films I wasn't in because you found my presence unwelcome," said the actress.

"Giulietta is my Beatrice," he said, turning upon his partner a sweet, disingenuous smile.

"The truth is we have divided duties between ourselves," the actress replied. "Federico rules supreme on the set; I in the home. But he has always made me pay for the sovereignty I exercise indoors. I have never loved myself: I am a dwarf with a little round face and bristly hair. Ever since he was preparing *La Strada* I have dreamed that Federico would give me the face of Garbo or Katharine Hepburn; instead he has made my face ever rounder and my hair ever more bristly and has shrunk me even more. He turned me into a punk *ante litteram.*"

"I made you more seductive than Jean Harlow or Marilyn Monroe," he said.

The actress riposted: "As you all know, Federico loves women who are monumental, curvaceous, sumptuous, but I, just because I am so little and skinny, managed to sneak in between those living statues, disguised in the clothes of Gelsomina, Cabiria, Juliet of the Spirits, Ginger, and thus enjoy my revenge on him."

The crowd exploded in thunderous applause and Fellini changed the subject, taking the opportunity to pay further tribute to Kurosawa. He described how he had seen *Dreams* again the previous evening at Sony's headquarters, and how he had been amazed anew by the sequence where Van Gogh, played by Martin Scorsese, enters one of his own paintings. He added: "It is a memorable sequence and, who knows, even I might decide to use High Definition."

Before they left for Kyoto, Fellini and Masina were invited by Kurosawa to Ten Masa, the restaurant in the Kanda area where the Emperor Hirohito used to lunch. As Fellini said later, "Hirohito, a god on earth, mysterious and inscrutable, would eat secretly at Ten Masa because he was fond of hot, crispy fish, whereas at the Imperial Palace the kitchen was a long way from the dining room and the fish always arrived cold. Even gods have their Achilles' heels. Dante would have consigned Hirohito to the infernal circle of the jealous."

In March 1993 I accompanied Fellini and Masina to Los Angeles. He had learned that the Motion Picture Academy had decided to award him an Oscar for his career on the very day of his seventy-third birthday, January 20, and had taken special pleasure in the coincidence. "It would be an unpardonable discourtesy if I were not to go to Hollywood this time to pick up the mythical statue in person," he had declared. And, despite suffering from cervical arthrosis, which occasionally made him dizzy, he had embarked in good spirits upon another long journey.

We boarded the plane at Leonardo da Vinci around two in the afternoon of March 26. In addition to Masina, the director was accompanied by Marcello Mastroianni, Rinaldo Geleng and his wife, his secretary Fiammetta Profili and the head of his press office, Mario Longardi (also on the plane was Gillo Pontecorvo, who had been invited to the Oscar ceremony as director of the Venice Film Festival). They were a little clan of artists and intimates who were welcomed everywhere, both in the airport and on the plane, with great affection. On board, Fellini refrained from getting up for fear of becoming dizzy; he wrote, sketched, made witty remarks and exchanged reminiscences with Masina and Mastroianni. "Federico,

I'm also suffering from dizzy spells: in the morning, when I get up, I feel like I'm walking on shifting sands, or on a carpet of eggs," the actor told him.

"It was a challenge, in my condition, to tackle this long journey: my head is spinning, I'm swaying," Fellini said under his breath just before he set foot on the tarmac around five in the evening local time, before the cameramen and news photographers fell upon him and the crowd exploded in loud applause.

"I've arrived like Groucho Marx, but it's still not time to retire," he added. Then he said, "I'm even prey to a kind of autosuggestion: the more I think about my cervical arthrosis, the more the discomfort increases, or at least so it seems to me; but now I'm happy to be here, I couldn't not pick up the Prize of Prizes in person, such a great recognition of all my work, if not all my life."

For the three days that Fellini spent in Los Angeles, the Beverly Hilton Hotel became the terminus of an incessant pilgrimage: all the Hollywood directors wanted to see him, speak to him, congratulate him, wish him long life and a speedy return to the set. But many of them could see him only during the afternoon of March 29, at the Dorothy Chandler Pavilion, the great theater where the Oscar presentation ceremony took place.

It is hard to forget Fellini's arrival with Masina and Mastroianni at the Pavilion. On two sides of a driveway covered with a red carpet, and on two enormous stairways which had been constructed on the left, were crowded more than two thousand news photographers and cameramen. "Federico!," "Giulietta!," "Marcello!" they yelled as the three went past, urging them to turn toward their lenses and maneuvering their equipment like weaponry. A dizzying, chaotic throng, an immense Babel, full of cars, trucks, panning floodlights, spotlights, a crowd in nervous motion, men in dinner jackets and women in evening gowns.

All the while in the gray skies helicopters whirled around at low altitude, vaguely menacing. Demonstrators from an extremist religious sect, overcome with puritan rage, were chanting that the cinema was the work of the devil and must be destroyed. The scene lasted for more than twenty minutes, until the illustrious guests at last reached the audience in the Pavilion. There had never been such an uproarious and delirious reception for any other director, screenwriter, actor, or actress. By a form of the law of retaliation, the director had himself suffered the kind of assault to which he had subjected Anita Ekberg in *La Dolce Vita,* although increased beyond all limits, beyond any cinematic invention.

The greatest, most emotional and triumphant moment of the whole ceremony came when, from the stage of the Pavilion, Fellini said to Masina, who was sitting in the seventh row of the orchestra, "Stop crying." The spotlights lit up the actress's face, wet with tears: the face of Gelsomina, the unforgettable character in *La Strada,* the film for which Fellini, way back in 1956, had won his first Oscar.

Conversations with Fellini

Growing up in Rimini

COSTANZO COSTANTINI: *Rimini: what does this word stir up in you?*

FEDERICO FELLINI: The memory of a train whistle, the train that used to carry my father back home around seven in the evening. I regret agreeing to talk about my birthplace. It seems to me that I have nothing to say. How does one manage to give an account of things that actually exist? I feel better when I'm inventing things. The real Rimini, where I passed the years of my childhood and adolescence, is mixed up with the other, imagined, re-created and reconstructed city in my films at Cinecittà or at ancient Viterbo and at Ostia. The two memories are superimposed upon each other and I can no longer tell the difference.

You don't have any memories of Rimini that are more precise, distinct and vivid than the others?
In summer, half-naked bodies which ran toward the sea under the huge dazzling sun, and a deafening torrent of sound made up of voices, music and the metallic tones of a loudspeaker which repeats the name of a little girl who has wandered away from her parents. And in the winter, the fog, which made everything disappear. What a thrill to be wrapped in the fog:

you became the invisible man; no one could see you and so you didn't exist.

Do you remember how you walked to school?
I don't remember the street names, but I do remember the war memorial near my junior school. A powerful, virile figure in bronze held out a dagger toward the heavens, while a naked woman representing glory reclined on one elbow, somewhat uncomfortably. Whenever it rained we would stand under umbrellas to watch her lovely big ass, which the water rendered so luminous and throbbing that she seemed alive. And then there were the steps of the gloomy schoolhouse—like a rickety skyscraper—which we would run up howling like Malay tiger cubs, only to be greeted by kicks up the backside by the headmaster. He was over six feet tall, bony and stooped, with a huge red beard: half fire-eater, half Zeus, he would try to crush us against the steps like cockroaches. My companions at high school were the same ones I had had from my earliest schooldays. The oldest one is now a famous criminal lawyer, highly respected by the judiciary, but when he was three he tried to murder me with a wooden spade as we both sat paddling at the seaside.

To when do your first childhood memories date back?
I was three or four. I remember the nuns of San Vincenzo who ran the nursery school I went to. How could I ever forget them, with their enormous hats? I also remember Giovannini, the master of Teatini primary school who made us sing "Youth, youth, the springtime of beauty," the Fascist anthem.

What were your favorite subjects?
In primary school I had started to doodle away while reading the *Corriere dei Piccoli* and then, later on, the tales of Salgari. I loved design and art history. I was always dashing off sketches,

caricatures and cartoons. In 1936, when I was sixteen, I produced a set of caricatures of the musketeers in the holiday camp at Verucchio, a mountain resort about twenty kilometers from Rimini. They were published the following year in *La Diana* by the Opera Balilla of Rimini. That was my first break as a designer and caricaturist. In the same year, in partnership with the painter Demos Bonini, I opened the Artist's Studio near the cathedral, where we did caricatures to order, even in people's homes. I did the designs and signed myself Fe; Demos added the color and signed himself Bo. We got ourselves a rubber stamp marked "Febo." But I also signed myself "Fellas"—who knows why.

Who taught you most about design and caricature?
My idea of the perfect caricaturist was Giuseppe Zarini, called Nino Za. Nino Za worked in Berlin drawing caricatures for the cover of *Lustige Blätter* magazine. You could get hold of it even in Rimini and I never failed to buy a copy at the station kiosk. Subsequently, Nino Za moved to Rimini, where he did caricatures on the terrace of the Grand Hotel. For me he was a legendary figure. He wore white trousers and a naval blazer and white gloves. He would see you only if you had made an appointment and never showed you what he was working on. Only when he had got his check would he hand over the caricature. He was a kind of international playboy in the world of caricature. But in Rimini I wasn't lucky enough to know him personally. I met him later in Rome and we became great friends.

So at that time you perhaps thought of becoming a painter?
Since I was little I had been fascinated by the figure of the painter and at that time there was a moment when I seriously thought that I would become one. I never thought I would end up as a scriptwriter and film director. Things were different

An unpublished photo of Fellini at age nine, taken at his family's home in Rimini. From left to right: Fellini's father, Fellini, his mother, his brother Riccardo, and his sister Maddalena (in their mother's arms). (D.R.)

then, but I've never stopped making designs and caricatures, and dashing off sketches of every kind. In 1937 and 1938 Carlo Massa, the owner of the Fulgor Cinema in Rimini, commissioned from me a series of caricatures of the film stars in vogue at the time, for publicity purposes.

At what age did you have your first sexual experience?
When I was six or seven. At that time we had a housemaid called Marcella. She was a girl with a touch of the animal in her. One day all the family—my father and mother, my brother, Riccardo, who was a year younger than me, and my sister, Maddalena, who was born in 1929—had gone out and I was left alone in the house because I had a temperature. My

mother had told Marcella to check it from time to time. I had dozed off when Marcella lifted up my nightshirt, took my little prick in her hands and put it in her mouth. Afterward she went into the kitchen and brought back an enormous aubergine, which she inserted between her thighs and began sliding backwards and forwards with her hand. Ever since, I have never been able to bring myself to eat aubergines.

And when did you have your first relationship?
At high school, but it was a long-distance, purely visual one. My high-school friends were the same ones I had had at junior school, and even at nursery school, such as Luigi Benzi (the "Titta" of *Amarcord*), Luigi Dolci and Mario Montinari. Luigi Benzi I've already mentioned: he is now the famous criminal lawyer. I was in love with "the eleven o'clock lady." At that hour the blinds of a balcony window opposite our classroom would open and there appeared in a dressing gown a beautiful woman who talked to her cat, to her caged canaries and to the flowers in her vases. When she leaned over to water the flowers, her dressing gown would open a little upon her breast. We would await this moment from half-past eight in the morning. Sometimes the math teacher, in his endless walking between the desks with his hands behind his back, would approach the window, seeking the object of our gazes, and would stay there to watch, going up and down on his toes.

But who was your actual "first love"?
Bianchina.

This Bianchina has become a myth, like Leopardi's Silvia.
She was real flesh and blood, a lovely girl called Bianchina Soriani. I even scrawled some drawings to express my love for her. I portrayed the two of us walking arm in arm down an avenue of trees, like Peynet's lovers, or watching from the end

of the pier the distant horizon toward Yugoslavia. In the seventies, Bianchina told her own story in a novel called *Una Vita in Più*.

And did you also write poetry for her?
No. I can't credit myself, or shame myself, with ever having written love poems. I've written all kinds: songs, odes, nursery rhymes, verse parodies, couplets for curtain-raising soubrettes, but I've never tried my hand at classical love poetry in the *dolce stil novo*.

Do you remember the first time you went to the cinema?
I think I've said this many times before: the first film I ever saw in the Fulgor Cinema, Rimini, was *Giant in Hell*. I was a toddler and stayed in my father's arms. The cinema was packed full and smoky. That film made such an impression on me that I've tried several times to remake it. In those days the cinema really was a ritualistic experience, like going to church, although church wasn't quite so packed and smoky. In church there was the priest, who, from the pulpit, thundered against sinners, calling up the forces of hell and threatening punishments which would strike before nightfall. In the cinema there was Mae West, who had her own kind of threats for the evening, if a little less alarming. I often tried to persuade Mae West to be in one of my films, but I never succeeded, just as I never managed to do a remake of *Giant in Hell*.

Did you go to the theater?
Extremely rarely. Going to the theater in Rimini meant seeing something that you wouldn't understand because you hadn't studied, because you were a scamp, a rascal, an incorrigible urchin. I studied little or nothing. On the few occasions I did go to the theater the teacher would threaten me: "If you don't keep quiet, I'll chuck you out." And they really did kick me

out—much to my delight, as I was more interested in seeing what was going on outside. What happened on the stage did not interest me particularly. I was fascinated by the overall effect, the magical character of the theater: the surroundings, the gardens, a train that could have decapitated a woman Grand Guignol-style, Louis XV speaking Bologna dialect. But I never followed the action; I wasn't gripped by what happened on the stage. Only the circuslike quality of the theater interested me. Notwithstanding that what I fundamentally do is theater, that the theater is the most congenial medium for Italians, and that in the theater I feel like a little boy in church who wants to become a priest, I didn't go to the theater and continue to not go. I enjoy being in the wings or on the stage, but it bores me to death to be in the audience. I'm much fonder of opera.

When did you first go to the opera?
When I was seven or eight. But my first contact with opera almost ended in tragedy. Dad was friends with a police commissioner called Chianese who looked like Ben Turpin. He used to play the tough guy and his reputation was sufficient to scare even the most hardened criminals. Actually he was a very gentle man with a morbid love of music, especially opera. He had a box at the Teatro Comunale and let my father use it. Once my father took me with him to see *I Cavalieri di Ekebú* by Zandonai. The box was right above the "mystic gulf" and you could see everything that went on in the wings: a bedlam of people in turmoil, huge women gargling with enormous colored glasses, singers who were shrieking. At the start of the opera the action took place in a fearful Nibelung cavern, the den of a malign deity like Vulcan or Wotan. There was a forge, a workshop for making weapons and a gigantic gong. The chorus of worker-demons chanted: "May thy thunder hammer fall, O horsemen of Ekebú." Then a massive drum descended, the

worker-demons emitted fierce yells and terrifying sounds came from the gong. I was dressed like Hamlet in a black velvet tunic with a white neck. All of a sudden my father noticed that the neck was stained with blood. The din had ruptured my eardrum and the blood had spurted onto my collar. I was taken straight to the hospital and it was a miracle that I wasn't left deaf for life.

Perhaps that's the reason why you don't much like music and have always refused to direct an opera?
I don't know. I don't think so. Opera, as I said, has always exercised a certain fascination over me, especially *Aida,* with which I have a particular relationship—intimate, I was about to say. In 1938 I appeared in *Aida* at the Baths of Caracalla in Rome along with my friend Rinaldo Geleng. We played the Numidian warriors who accompanied Amonasro, father of Aida. We got five lire a show. Our biggest problem was to avoid getting our tennis shoes covered in the big, loose balls of dung redolent of spinach that the elephants scattered all over the stage. But if I sense a certain attraction to the opera, I feel nothing toward the theater. Apart from anything else, I never manage to concentrate.

That's strange for a director like you, gifted with such acute powers of concentration.
I love all the preliminaries to an evening at the theater: the foyer, the masks, meeting an old friend, the boxes, the ringing of the bell, the dimmer lights gradually fading, the darkness, the silence, the coughing, the raising of the curtain. But when someone makes their entrance on the stage and begins moving about and talking, I'm gripped by the impulse to escape. But in spite of this impulse, the audience attracts me: they are like a swarm of jellyfish or schoolchildren forced to sit quietly, hardly breathing and holding back their sneezes. The truth is

that at school we suffered a kind of cultural terrorism: reading Aeschylus, Sophocles and Euripides in Greek traumatized us for life.

Have you ever been tempted to do some theater?
Yes, but not as a director; more likely as the moving spirit behind a happening, like the medium at a séance or the ringleader of a crew of comics. Even when, much later, I began to follow troupes of strolling players, what fascinated me was not the performance itself, but the train journeys, the stations, the flings with hotel waitresses, the hotels.

In 1938 you left high school and moved to Florence before establishing yourself in Rome. What images of Rimini did you carry with you when you left the city?
Those huge lips of the wife of the Savignano stationmaster, who gave me my first real kiss.

Those lips weren't an image of Rimini.
One memory I did take away with me was of the Rocca Malatestiana, a squat and gloomy prison fortress, full of menace. Under the battlements, through the dark embrasures one could make out hands manacled to the iron bars and the voices of the prisoners howling, "Do you have a cigarette?" They were twenty meters above the ground and we might have been able to climb up to them, but we were afraid they might grab hold of us and drag us inside. The circus used to pitch its tents in the square beneath the Rocca. In the summer they would take down the big top and the prisoners could follow the action, shrieking abuse at the acrobats and horsewomen.

Did this give you the idea for The Clowns?
Yes, this is the incident I recount at the beginning of that little film. But Rimini features not only in *I Vitelloni, La Strada,*

Amarcord and *Roma,* but even in those films which have no points of reference to my native town, like *La Dolce Vita, Satyricon, Casanova. And the Ship Sails On,* where the action always takes place against the distant backdrop of the sea—like a primordial element, a blue line cutting across the sky—whence arrive the pirate ships, the Turks, the King, the American battle cruisers with Ginger Rogers and Fred Astaire dancing in the shadow of the guns.

Which details of Rimini and which characters gave you the inspiration for I Vitelloni?
The youths we used to watch with admiration through the windows of the Bar Ausonia playing billiards in their camel-hair coats, colored shoes and sharp haircuts. They would take a long draw from a cigarette, then, letting the smoke out of their noses with all the formality of an immutable ritual, would slowly chalk their cues and, with elbow raised, would stretch their upper body over the billiard table and take repeated aim at the billiard ball. A solemn moment. Then the loud cracks of the ivory balls reached us in the street and one of us would applaud.

But couldn't you get past those windows for a closer view?
Only occasionally did they allow you to be present at the matches, to replace the fallen pegs and, a privilege even more gratifying, to mark the score. They were the same young men, with brooches under their tie-knots, whom I sometimes saw in a semicircle around a car of unknown make, discoursing gravely on its power and speed until the owner of the marvel turned up wearing big glasses and arm in arm with a woman wrapped in flashy furs.

Some say the idea for the film came from Ennio Flaiano, who knew this type of young man in the cafés of Pescara.

II

He had also known a similar type in Pescara, but the idea for the film wasn't his.

Does Zampanò in La Strada *also recall one of the characters you had known in Rimini as a boy?*
In part he recalls the gypsies, the Carbonari and the men who castrated the pigs whom I used to see in Gambettola, the place between Rimini and Cesena where we spent the summer. They were on their way to the mountains of Abruzzo. The pig-castrator arrived along the wide road in the evening, his knives gleaming on a bloodstained cloth. He boasted that he had had every woman in the area and related how he had got a poor mad girl pregnant who gave birth to a baby everyone called the son of the devil.

The monster who appears at the end of La Dolce Vita: *what memories inspired that?*
Also ones of Rimini. One morning, opening the windows, the girl who stayed with us exclaimed, "What is that terrible smell?" And we all stuck our noses out to have a sniff. The air was terrible with the stink of rotting flesh, as if thousands of tombs had been opened up. The body of an enormous sea monster had been washed up on the beach during the night and was polluting the area. That morning there were no lessons in school: teachers, headmasters, pupils—all had gone to the sea to see the monster. There was already a big crowd gathered: police, carabinieri, soldiers surrounded the hideous heap of rotting flesh. The headmaster asked sternly of the natural science teacher, "Professor Quaglianilo, in your opinion, what kind of fish is this?" "How the hell do I know?" he replied, to the applause of the schoolchildren. The fishermen who had begun to demolish the carcass with hatchets declared with a knowledgeable air that it was a "ray" from the north. The *Domenica*

del Corriere reproduced the scene on the front page with a drawing by Achille Beltrame.

You surely can't have forgotten the Grand Hotel?
As small boys in our little jackets and knickerbockers, the Grand Hotel in Rimini seemed like an enchanted palace, a symbol of luxury, of splendor and the fabulous Orient. We would dart around like squirrels to steal a peek at what was happening inside or on the terraces, where we could hear the theme tunes of the American films we had seen at the Fulgor during the winter, like *Sonny Boy, I Love You,* or *Alone.* On summer evenings, the Grand Hotel would be transformed in our boyish imaginations into Baghdad, Istanbul, Nineveh, Babylon, Hollywood. On its terraces, freshened by sea breezes, parties were held like those imagined by Ziegfeld. Women with magnificent breasts and half-naked backs could be glimpsed dancing with men in white tuxedos. In a word, the Grand Hotel was like the *Thousand and One Nights* for us.

Why have you never shot any of your films in Rimini, not even Amarcord?
Memory is by its nature an altered version of reality, a mediated view of what really happened. To relate stories, characters, encounters, passions that have been filtered through the memory is to express something which, in order to be faithful to the emotions and sentiments it stirs up, must be enriched with sounds, lights, colors, atmosphere. All this can be re-created only in that magical laboratory that, for the film-maker, is the studio. In Studio 5 of Cinecittà I re-created everything.

How did Rimini strike you in 1946, when you returned for the first time?
It was "rich in rubble" as my friends at *Marc' Aurelio* described Italy at the time. A lunar landscape; a blasted expanse of ruins.

After Cassino, it was the most bombed city in Italy. From that terrible ocean of destruction all that came forth into the clear, blue air was the dialect, the old cadence, and a voice calling out the family names I no longer heard in Rome: "Duilio, Severino . . ."

In 1955 you went back to Rimini after the death of your father, Urbano. How did you remember him and how do you remember him now?

As when I was a child: how else can one remember one's own parents? Who can honestly say that they knew their mother and father as real human beings? Only at his funeral did I seem to see my father as perhaps the man he would have been. Among the mourners were two or three comely, maternal, sensual women who looked as if they had fond memories of my father. They were weeping and their handkerchiefs were covered in mascara and lipstick. That sight made me understand that he had been a good and true friend.

Is it true that you had intended to make a film based on an incident connected with your father's funeral?

Yes, but it's an incident that I don't remember with pleasure. My sister, Maddalena, had telephoned to tell me that our father was ill. I was somewhat reckless in those days and instead of Giulietta I took a pretty girl with me to Rimini. I left her in a little hotel and went to see my father. Because his condition didn't appear too serious, I went for a bite to eat in a restaurant. All of a sudden a cab driver ran in and said to me, "Signor Fellini, Signor Fellini, come at once, your father is very ill." I rushed to the house, but when I got there my father was already dead. I was very distressed. I had to console my mother, organize the funeral and see to the arrangements. So I forgot all about the pretty girl who was waiting for me in the hotel. When I finally got back to her, she didn't want to have anything to do with me and I had to resort to every stratagem to placate her. Later, overcome by the memory of this sad incident, I thought about depicting it in a film. I even had a lead actress in mind, Sophia Loren, to play the part of the pretty girl. Dino De Laurentiis was to have been the producer. I even went to Los Angeles to talk to Gregory Peck, who was to be the lead actor. And I already had the title: *Viaggio con Anita*. But Giulietta wrote me a letter explaining the reasons why I could never make that film and so I gave it up, without another thought.

And your mother, who died in 1984: how do you remember her?
My parents were fair toward me and were just the kind I needed. Perhaps they were disappointed that I didn't become a lawyer or engineer as they had hoped, but they never opposed me and I was able to choose my own way without any friction and without having to justify myself. I may have caused my mother much displeasure, but the scandal that accompanied *La Dolce Vita* saddened and mortified her above all else. My mother was a devout woman, very religious, and the fact that her son had made a film that the Church condemned caused her deep suffering. The archbishop, who was already ancient when I was still at primary school, was severe in his strictures of the film and its creator, the son of Signora Ida Barbiani.

What did you do to comfort her?
Because it was beginning to make my mother ill, I went to Rimini to speak to the exalted prelate. He lived in a lovely seicento palazzo. As we came out of primary school at midday, we would sometimes see him as he passed through the elegant colonnade of the first floor in the company of two junior priests. We would yell at him like pirates, "Blessing! Blessing!" From his height he would slowly trace the sign of the cross in the air, while beneath him, with exaggerated jumps and much

genuflection, we asked for an encore. "You can have only a brief audience," his secretary said when I explained why I wanted to see the archbishop. "He is almost ninety, and is completely deaf." It pained me to raise my voice when talking about such delicate and private matters, but I forced myself and shouted as if I was at a rally in the town square. The young secretary, with his robust mountain-dweller's physique, bent down to the trembling old man and then, obviously lying and a little embarrassed, informed me that the archbishop had said, "Bravo, bravo." Then he added that he had liked the film a lot and that a mariner cousin of his had been to Sweden, the homeland of Anita Ekberg.

Since the deaths of your parents have you felt more detached from Rimini?
I have fewer reasons for going back. Only my sister, Maddalena, remains there, a very kind woman. I remember when she was born. I held her in my arms with trepidation, fearful lest she slip out of my hands. Now she is a big, stout woman. One night, as we were walking together along a street in Rome, she pointed at my shadow on the ground and said, "Federico, you look like Daddy."

How do you find present-day Rimini?
Hotels, bars, sandwich bars, nightclubs, discotheques as big as spaceships, thousands and thousands of people who take it by storm in the summer. Las Vegas is tranquil and quiet compared to Rimini: an unending procession of shiny cars; a kind of Milky Way made up of headlights.

Does nothing remain of the Rimini of your boyhood?
The squares, the monuments, the streets, the Arch of Augustus, the Bridge of Tiberius, the Grand Hotel. In the glare of the sun or in the grayness of the fog, the Grand Hotel is always

there, symbol of the exotic and the opulent, of beautiful women. It possesses something magical, mythical, outside of time.

You don't feel homesick?
For a long time my feelings about Rimini were confused. I never went back willingly, even to check an imaginary location. By then I had framed it in a certain aesthetic way and actual reencounters would have upset me. The imaginary Rimini had become the material for my work. The real Rimini was quite another matter. I was aware that, working like this, the symbolic image was at risk of becoming static, calcified, but this awareness impelled me to keep it alive. It is stupid to destroy symbols on the pretext that they are the fruit of a reactionary attachment. Cinema is a living medium when it forces the filmmaker to make the symbols by which he expresses himself come alive.

But these days do you return to Rimini willingly?
For some years now I have felt a stronger nostalgia for Rimini. It's like a sweet sickness. Without being aware of it, I find myself thinking of Rimini, of the Rimini of my childhood and adolescence, of my first amorous forays. I succumb more and more to a typical *vitellone* fantasy: to go and stay for a few days at the Grand Hotel and sleep in the Stanza della Gradisca or the Stanza del Principe.

What does it mean to you to be a romagnolo?*
The word Romagna suggests to me something warm, protective, sensual. It makes me think of a gentle, affectionate, nour-

---

* Speaker of the dialect of the Emilia-Romagna region.

ishing, but unknown mother. I say it with a sense of guilt, but I don't really know Romagna. Every time I'm away from Rome I feel this. We filmmakers have said almost nothing about Italy. Our country is still an unknown universe.

An Artist's Adolescence

In spite of everything that Fellini has told about himself and that others have written about him, his childhood and adolescence remain largely unexplored. In particular, not enough is known about his work as a designer, caricaturist and vignettist, or even as a painter. But now evidence is emerging that he was something of a true "child prodigy." Documents recently discovered allow one to reconstruct what could be called "a portrait of the artist as a young man," or, paraphrasing the title of Joyce's work, "a portrait of the young man as an artist," or even "a portrait of Fellini through his drawings, caricatures, vignettes and pictures."

These documents reveal that, in addition to Demos Bonini and Nino Za, another caricaturist who influenced Fellini was Italo Roberti. He was a violinist who played in Rimini at the Grand Hotel and the casino during the summer, as well as in the little band at the Fulgor Cinema, which, before the advent of sound, would underscore the moments of high emotion in the film. Italo Roberti, like Fellini, had learned to make drawings and caricatures by observing those of Nino Za, the typically Riminese caricaturist who put down everything that caught his eye during the summer when the whole town became a kind of open-air theater. Caricature was the cultural expression of that ephemeral season by the seaside. He even sketched the projectionist at the Fulgor Cinema, Giovanni Lucchi, who died in 1947. The series of caricatures of actors and actresses which Fellini executed for the owner of the Fulgor must have been extensive, judging by the thirty or so recently discovered, including those of George Murphy, Herbert Marshall and Ruby Dalmas, an actress who was quite famous at the time. Her caricature bears in the bottom left-hand corner the words "To the artist Fellini, Ruby

*Departure and separation, 1939: Fellini (left) with
Luigi Benzi, Mario Montanari, and Luigi Dolci.*

Dalmas," a dedication from her to him and not vice versa. They are
all signed "Fellas."

Some recently discovered photographs are also very interesting.
Fellini had always said that during his childhood and adolescence
in Rimini he never wore a bathing suit because he was embarrassed at being as thin as a rake. "I have never worn a swimsuit
in my life, not in Rimini, not in Fregene, not in Ostia, nor anywhere
else," he used to say. But a photograph taken in 1975 shows him
in a swimsuit on the beach at Rimini with Luigi Benzi and Mario
Montanari. He also appears with Benzi, Montanari and Luigi Dolci
in a photograph taken in 1939. It is a souvenir, a picture of departure and separation. His three friends leave together for Bologna to

Caricatures: Alessandro Campi and Herbert Marshall.

enroll at the university, from which all three graduate in law. At the same time, Fellini leaves for Rome to enroll at that unique kind of university, the *Marc' Aurelio,* one of the most famous humor magazines of the period.

Caricatures: George Murphy and Ruby Dalmas.

Part of a series of caricatures executed by Fellini in Rimini in 1936–37: Three sisters from Rimini go to Sicily to find husbands but return empty-handed.

Rome, Cinecittà, Giulietta Masina

COSTANZO COSTANTINI: *Why did you quit Rimini for Florence in 1938?*

FEDERICO FELLINI: I had been to Florence before, just as I had been to Rome. I used to go to the editorial offices of *420* and *Avventuroso,* two magazines published by Società Nerbini which I did some work for. After high school, I stayed there for six or seven months, after which I moved to Rome.

When was your first trip to Rome?

In 1933 or 1934, with my father. My mother came from Rome and one of her brothers, Alfredo Barbiani, took me in his car on a tour of the city. Looking out of the window he said to me, "This is the Colosseum . . . This is Castel St. Angelo . . . This is the Garibaldi Monument." I felt like I was at school, bewildered by the dizzying succession of columns and statues and immense ruins. At the Trevi Fountain, at the Pincio, at Piazza Navona we took some snapshots. That first tour round the wonders of Rome also had its moment of drama: I got lost in the catacombs of San Callisto. The guides shouted, "Boy from Rimini lost in the catacombs!" The nightmare lasted for about a quarter of an hour.

But how did Rome strike you when you were eighteen or nineteen?
One of the things I found most striking was the monumental
rudeness that I encountered everywhere. A gigantic rudeness
and a gigantic vulgarity. This vulgarity is part of the character
of Rome, that magnificent vulgarity to which the Latin authors
have left testimony—Plautus, Martial, Juvenal. It is the vulgarity of Petronius's *Satyricon*. It is a kind of liberation, a vic-
tory over the fear of bad taste, over propriety. For anyone who
observes the city with the aim of expressing it creatively, the
vulgarity is an enrichment, an aspect of the fascination that
Rome inspires. But Rome seemed to me immediately a familiar, welcoming and friendly city—perhaps because my mother
was a Roman.

Where did you live when you arrived in Rome?
In Via Albalonga, in a bed-sitter my father had found for me,
through friends in Rimini.

Aldo Fabrizi, the great actor in Rossellini's Rome, Open City,
*said you lived in Via Sannio, not in Via Albalonga, and that
before that you had long been his guest in Via Germanico, near
St. Peter's.*
Yes, yes, I also lived near the Vatican. When I had a little
money I would take a cab home, sometimes sitting beside the
driver, admiring the façades of the churches, the bridges, the
statues on the bridges, the cornices of the patrician palazzi.
Occasionally I would ask the cab driver to take me to St.
Peter's, the sight of which always fascinated me: the basilica
has an almost ethereal lightness, which one finds in no other
architecture. I was able to treat myself to cabs from time to
time because I did articles, interviews, short stories and caricatures for *Il Piccolo, Marc' Aurelio* and other periodicals.

Rinaldo Geleng has described how, when he knew you in 1938–39, you didn't even have the money for two rice croquettes. He says he was looking at a tray of steaming rice croquettes in the window of a deli in Via Regina Elena, near the offices of Marc' Aurelio, *when you appeared alongside him like a long black shadow, like a specter, and asked him, although you had never seen him before, "How much money have you got? I've just enough for one, and you?"*

We weren't in Via Regina Elena, the present-day Via Barberini, but near the Casa del Passeggero, and the deli was called Canepa.

Geleng replied that the rice croquettes cost sixpence each and he had enough for four. But when you both went into the shop, you told him that you couldn't find your money and had probably left it in another jacket. "You really have another jacket?" Geleng asked you, and paid for the four croquettes, two for each of you. Is this true?

Yes, it's true. We looked like Charlie Chaplin and Buster Keaton. But afterward I made him a millionaire. I gave him work on my films, as well as his two sons, Antonello and Giuliano, the first as a production designer, the second as a painter, like his father.

Geleng also recounts how you left hotels during the night without paying the bill.

But where, and when? That day we met I had an appointment with Stefario Vanzina—the future director Steno—who was the editorial secretary of *Marc' Aurelio.* Thanks to him, I began to work permanently at *Marc' Aurelio,* writing treatments and screenplays for the actors Macario and Aldo Fabrizi, and for RAI.

But all this happened a lot later. Geleng recalls that one day he, you and the scriptwriter Ruggero Maccari—along with the journalist Luigi Garrone and another of your friends—all went for lunch to a trattoria in Via del Boschetto, although you knew that not one of you had any money. Is that true?

Yes, we used to go to those restaurants where we knew intuitively that we could eat for free without the management calling the cops. That day not one of us had the courage to tell the owner that we hadn't a penny. It was almost four o'clock when I decided to send him a note. "We are five 'brothers,' but we don't have any money." After he had read it, the owner, who looked like Chaplin, with his trembling legs, asked us, "Would the gentlemen also like to stay for dinner?"

Geleng recalls that one of the hotels from which you did a run at night, lowering your suitcases by a rope out of the window, was the Esperia in Via Nazionale.

I honestly don't remember this. But I repeat that it was thanks to Carzina, Fabrizi and the scriptwriter Piero Tellini that I began to work in film and television.

Do you remember where you met Aldo Fabrizi?

I met him at the Corso Cinema, where he was doing an open-air show. At that time I used to go to the theaters that showed revues and curtain-raisers, such as the Volturno, the Fenice, the Brancaccio, the Alcione—but only to pass on gags to the actors in the wings. I rarely watched the shows. But I did see that one of Fabrizi's. At the end I went up to him to give him my compliments and we became friends.

Fabrizi said that in the evenings you would accompany him to his house in Via Sannio. You got him to tell you everything that

happened to him during the day and then used it in your treatments and screenplays.
What details of his stories?

He cited the pose with outstretched arm—"Up yours!"—which you had Alberto Sordi adopt in I vitelloni. *He said that this was really his gesture. He was on his way to a wedding reception; there was a group of laborers working by the roadside. He gestured to them "Up yours!" They chased him with their shovels and he had to seek refuge in a field of tomatoes.*
Aldo Fabrizi was a wonderful friend to me when I was new in Rome. I was very fond of him. I stood godfather at the christenings of both his children, Massino and Vilma. And of course I took note of the tales he told me, they were so amusing! But I don't remember if I got that gesture with the outstretched arm from him.

He said that when you made L'ultima carrozzella *you had wanted to have the horse talking and he said to you, "Freddy, do you really want to have a talking horse? How could you have such a crazy idea?!"*
If Caligula could make his horse a senator, why couldn't I make one speak?

Fabrizi said that you forgot him when you became famous and shifted your enthusiasm onto Marcello Mastroianni. He recounts how one day he met you in Via del Babuino and said, with reference to that famous gesture, "What the hell are you doing? You put something of mine in your film without acknowledging me?"
I'm sorry I didn't ask him to be in *Satyricon,* but I wanted to make a totally imaginary film, outside of time, and his presence would have instilled an overrealistic quality. Fabrizi was a very precious guiding figure for me through the Inferno, like a

good-natured Charon. It was through him that I began really to understand the Roman character and the life of the people in the suburbs. I remember an evening at that time that I spent with a lower-middle-class family. The head of the family was an office worker. Well, after dinner he said, "Now we'll go and see Rome." And they went to see Rome as if they were going to a show. In which other city would such a thing happen? I've never heard people in Milan say, "Now we'll go and see Milan." It's not even said in Venice, that supremely theatrical city.

Where, how and when did you meet Giulietta Masina?
Giulietta Masina was the woman of my destiny. I've come to believe that our relationship really existed before the day we met for the first time.

But when, where and how did you meet each other?
Giulietta has told the story many times. It's well known. All the same, we met in 1942 at the headquarters of Italian Radio. After that first meeting we had lunch together in the center of Rome, in Piazza Poli, where Gogol lived. The restaurant was called Castaldi. That's how we began to see each other and a year later we got married.

In the drawing you made for the wedding invitation, which took place on October 30, 1943, you also put your addresses. Giulietta lived at 2 Via Lutezia in the Parioli quarter and you lived at 26 Via Nicotera in the Prati quarter. Why did you go to live at her place and not the other way round?
Because in my bed-sitter there was scarcely room for me and my suitcases. I hardly lived in a palace.

And yet Giulietta says that the first time you asked her out to dinner she was astonished at the amount of money you spent and the enormous tip you gave the waiters.

In 1942 I was already doing some work for cinema, as well as working for *Marc' Aurelio* and other magazines. With Piero Tellini I wrote *Documento Z₃*, directed by Alfredo Guarini and starring Isa Miranda. Still with Tellini and also with Cesare Zavattini I wrote *Avanti c'è posto*, starring Aldo Fabrizi.

Do you remember where you and Giulietta went for a honeymoon?

To Piazza Colonna, in the historic center of Rome. Alberto Sordi was doing a variety show at the Galleria Theater. We had scarcely taken our seats when Sordi asked the orchestra for a brief silence and invited the audience to give us a round of applause. Not that we were that well off in 1943. I remember I took to writing down in a diary all that happened to us. A while ago Giulietta reminded me of some of the things I wrote in it. The diary had monthly entries. January 1944: "This month we have earned only ten lire." February: "We have earned less than last month." March: "Fortunately the Germans didn't capture me." To tell the truth, they had apprehended me, but I managed to escape. They captured me in Piazza di Spagna, where I had gone looking for the screenwriter Sergio Amidei. They put me in a truck. While we were going along the Via del Babuino, the truck slowed down to let a German official go past. I started shouting to him "Fritz! Fritz!" as if I knew him and made as if to greet him. Then I slipped down a side street and escaped. I got back home much later than usual and found Giulietta with her heart in her mouth, afraid that something had happened to me. But if I escaped, I'm afraid that Michelina—the little dog I gave to Giulietta— didn't manage to save herself. She ended up under a German tank in Via Liegi, near our house. A few days later I picked up a stray dog in the street and carried it home to her. We called him Pasqualino, I don't remember why.

Didn't you manage to do any work during the occupation of Rome? The months of the German occupation of Rome—September 1943 to June 1944—were very hard, not only for Giulietta and me, but for everybody. However, I managed to do some work. I worked on two more of Fabrizi's films: *Campo de'fiori,* directed by Mario Bonnard, and *L'ultima carrozzella,* directed by Mario Mattoli. I also wrote some bits and pieces for another two or three short films. I used to go into restaurants to see if the customers wanted their caricatures done, although I had to be very careful because I was dodging conscription and they were looking for me. But after June 1944 everything changed. With Enrico De Seta and other friends from *Marc' Aurelio* we opened a studio to do caricatures for the Allied soldiers. We called it "Funny Face Shop: Profiles, Portraits, Caricatures." We made up vignettes, scenes from ancient Roman history, leaving blank the space for the head or profile of the client. We worked without respite. We had never seen so much money before.

An Imaginary Biography

Fellini's stories do not always tally with those of his biographers and friends. The discrepancies are sometimes striking. When he is contradicted, the director insists that his version is "the truth." And the reason is not hard to grasp. Although a very acute observer of the real world and despite his extraordinary memory, Fellini has constructed for himself a kind of imaginary biography—what some might call a "mythobiography"—and is intolerant of those who want to change it, reluctant to accept different versions of this or that event.

Fellini portrays himself as a badly behaved ragamuffin, whereas it is clear that he was a good and sweet-natured little boy. He represents himself as a very poor pupil, good only at drawing and doing "doodles," whereas it emerges that in his second year at high school he got excellent marks in almost all subjects.

Illustrative of this kind of discrepancy is the story of the two years of primary education—the third and fourth—that Fellini should have spent as a boarder at the ecclesiastical college of the Padri Carissimi in Fano, a famous town in the Marches. The chronology published in 1985 for the international seminar on Fellini in Seville states: "1927. My primary education in a religious college in Fano. Deep resentment at the hard regime. Religious traumas caused by the arduous rituals." But as Tullio Kezich writes in his biography of Fellini: "One must acknowledge the fact that Fellini never went to this college. His brother Riccardo was sent there and perhaps Fellini experienced the harshness of the discipline and the religious traumas by proxy through his brother's descriptions." All the same, Fellini maintains that it was he who went there, to the extent that he introduced the episode into 8½.

Roberto Rossellini, *Variety Lights,*
The White Sheik, I Vitelloni, La Strada,
The Nights of Cabiria

COSTANZO COSTANTINI: *Roberto Rossellini is the only film-maker whom you have acknowledged as a mentor. How did your relationship with him begin and develop?*

FEDERICO FELLINI: If I remember correctly, I met him at Aci Films, a film company whose patron was Vittorio Mussolini, one of the sons of the Fascist head of state. I saw him again in one of the Scalera Studios when I was interviewing Greta Honda for *Cinemagazzino*. But our first proper meeting was in the Funny Face Shop in Via Nazionale. I was working on a profile when there emerged, from the crowd of Allied soldiers, a middle-class type with a wide-brimmed hat and a pointed chin. It was Roberto Rossellini. He had come to ask me to work on the screenplay for his life of Don Morosini, the parish priest of Santa Melania who was murdered by an SS firing squad—in other words, on *Rome, Open City*. Rossellini had thought of me because he knew I was a friend of Aldo Fabrizi, whom he wanted for the part of Don Morosini, and hoped that I might persuade the actor to accept it without asking too high a fee.

How was Rome, Open City *received?*
Initially with great reservations, especially by the critics. But

later it enjoyed great popularity, first in Italy and th
It became one of the key films of what was later c
realism. Because of my involvement in the script of *Ro*
City, my name became associated with those directo who
defined that great period of Italian cinema.

*What do you remember of your first experience behind the camera
as Rossellini's assistant director on* Paisà?
It was a very important experience for me. Rossellini was the
originator of open-air cinema, working in the midst of ordinary
people, in the most unpredictable circumstances. It was by ac-
companying him as he shot *Paisà* that I discovered Italy. From
him I derived the conception of film as journey, adventure,
odyssey. He was a peerless friend and teacher to me. Giulietta
also had a small part in *Paisà*, little more than one scene, but
a valuable experience for her all the same. *Paisà* is one of the
most beautiful films in the history of cinema. It has the epic
quality of Homer, solemn as a Gregorian chant. In six discrete
episodes the author portrays, in a powerful and harrowing style,
Italy emerging from the havoc of war. I'm not saying this
merely because I was involved, with Sergio Amidei, in writing
the treatment and screenplay, but because I'm really convinced
of it. After *Paisà*, I wrote for Rossellini, in association with
Tullio Pinelli, the treatments for *The Miracle* and *The Countess
of Montecristo*. *The Miracle* was one of the two parts of *The
Ways of Love*, the other being *The Human Voice*, based on Jean
Cocteau's one-act play. The lead actress was Magnani; indeed
all his films were a kind of homage paid by Roberto to Anna
Magnani.

Is it true that The Miracle *was also inspired by your memories of
childhood and adolescence?*
There was a story with similarities to the one I told about the
pig-castrator. It concerned a mad shepherdess who falls in love

with a shepherd, mistaking him for St. Joseph. She becomes pregnant and, with the burden in her womb, climbs to the summit of a mountain where there is a tiny church. In the narrow confines of the bell tower she gives birth. She thinks the baby is the infant Jesus—whereas the woman made pregnant by the pig-castrator thought she had brought a little devil into the world. I even played the part of the Joseph figure, as a peroxide blond. I also worked with Rossellini on the selection of *The Flowers of Saint Francis.*

What were Rossellini's main characteristics?
As I have said on other occasions, he was a unique, unpredictable genius. For me, neorealism is identified with Rossellini. From *Rome, Open City* to *The Flowers of Saint Francis* Rossellini achieved a decisive leap forward in the history of cinema.

How did you get your first break as a director, or codirector, for Variety Lights?
Pinelli and I did screenplays for a multitude of films: *Il delitto di Giovanni Episcopo, Senza pietà* and *Il mulino del Po* directed by Alberto Lattuada; *Il passatore* by Duilio Coletti; *In nome della legge, Il cammino della speranza, Il brigante di Tacca del Lupo* and *La città si difende* by Pietro Germi. But even before Lattuada invited me to codirect *Variety Lights,* I had already had a little directing experience. The producer Luigi Rovere had given Gianni Puccini his directorial debut in *Persiane chiuse,* a film written by me and Pinelli and set in Turin. But after a few days on the set, Puccini suffered a kind of breakdown. Rovere suggested I take his place, but I proposed Luigi Comencini. Before Comencini arrived, so as not to delay the production, I shot a scene in which the police find a body in the Po. Rovere was very pleased with this scene and it was he who later asked me to direct *The White Sheik.*

How was Variety Lights *born?*

It was inspired by my memories of touring Italy with a variety show, of the countryside glimpsed from train windows, of the people observed from the wings of dilapidated and ill-lit provincial theaters. Pinelli, Lattuada and I wrote the screenplay in collaboration with Ennio Flaiano. To finance it we formed a cooperative, consisting of me and Giulietta, Lattuada and his wife, the actress Carla Del Poggio. The principal actors were Giulietta, Carla, Peppino De Filippo, Folco Lulli, Franca Valeri; there was also Sophia Loren, who was then called Sofia Lazzaro. I remember that Sophia came to see me with her mother. I asked her to do a screen test. She was thin, very thin, but she had a magnificent chest. She was wearing a blouse with a zip fastening. As I moved around, her mother suddenly pulled down the zipper and her breasts burst out.

The producer, who was named Mario Langhirani, covered part of the cost; the rest was paid by the cooperative. But producers didn't take kindly to this initiative of ours and made life difficult for us in every way imaginable. Carlo Ponti even produced a spoiler, *A Dog's Life,* with Aldo Fabrizi.

How did the codirecting go?
To tell the truth, Lattuada did everything, I just looked on.

Was the film a hit?
We're still paying the bills.

The White Sheik, *the film with which you really began your career as a director in 1952—did that go better?*
It was an extremely adventurous debut. The film—from a treatment by Michelangelo Antonioni and with a script written by me, Pinelli and Flaiano—called for a scene to be shot in the middle of the sea. There was a little boat tied to a raft on which we deployed the camera and floodlights; the raft, in turn,

was attached to a huge metal hull; the huge metal hull fastened to a pontoon where the crew and cast were. This whole crocodile contraption was in the sea at Fiumicino, where I was expected for the first setup in my life and where I arrived late. A launch carried me out to sea: the sea seemed motionless, but slyly and treacherously it shifted continually. In the bat of an eyelid the setup, which had been so meticulously prepared, was lost from the viewfinder forever. Where the sky had been was now the beach; instead of the pontoon with the actors on it, there was a pier. I didn't shoot a thing that day. It was a disaster, I was a failure. That was the unhappiest night of my life.

What happened afterward?
The following day we all moved with the cast to Fregene. We pitched camp in a space in Villaggio dei Pescatori where there was a little cabin with some boats. The manager was a fisherman named Ignazio Mastino who came from Sardinia. He had come to the Roman coast between Ostia and Fregene in the thirties, attracted by rumors that the waters were rich in fish. Ignazio was a kind of olive tree, a tree scorched by the salt sea air. We hired the boats and I gave him a small part in the film. I had one boat with the leading actors—Alberto Sordi and Brunella Bovo—placed on the shoreline. I had a hole dug in the sand, I put the camera into it and shot the scene on dry land.

What other scenes in the film were set in Fregene?
The scene of the swing in the pine forest, but both Sordi and I have told the tale many times, both nobly trying to outdo the other in inventing preposterous exaggerations.

What do you recall of the reactions the film provoked at the Venice Film Festival?

It was a disaster. I got such a drubbing that I lost the will to go on.

But fortunately you did persevere.
The film was screened in the afternoon, when people usually had a siesta, especially in the summer. Occasionally I heard applause, but I found it hard to believe it was real. If everyone in the audience boos and only one person applauds, the author, strange to say, hears only the cheers of that solitary spectator. In fact, in the days that followed I was destroyed, demolished. Nino Ghelli, in *Bianco e Nero,* was the fiercest critic. Only Giancarlo Fusco, Pietro Bianchi, Tullio Kezich and Vittorio Bonicelli wrote well of the film, but their words were drowned in a sea of insults. The film was destroyed, strangled at birth. For one or two days it remained in a few cinemas, then it disappeared. The public refused to see it because they detested Alberto Sordi. They didn't understand him, they couldn't bear his impudence. They loathed that little seminarist's voice in that heavy, fat-assed body.

But the following year in Venice there was a better reception for I Vitelloni?
The film won the Golden Lion, but to bring it to the screen I had to overcome enormous difficulties. As a kind of challenge to the public I reengaged Alberto Sordi. Three-quarters of the way through the film, the producer ran out of money. No one wanted to distribute it. ENIC ordered that Sordi's name not appear in the credits or on the posters. The RKO delegate lapsed into a profound slumber during a private screening of the film, and when the lights went up asked me, "Can you tell me how it ended?"

With La Strada, *in 1954, Venice really made it up to you?*
La Strada obtained another Golden Lion and enjoyed much

greater success than *Vitelloni*. But afterward the critics got their own back with *Il Bidone*, attacking it fiercely. Perhaps they were disconcerted by the harsh tone of the film, but they weren't very gentle all the same.

With La Strada *you won your first Oscar. What do you remember of the ceremony in Hollywood?*
We rehearsed in the Chinese Theater in Beverly Hills. Sunset Boulevard seemed covered in gold dust. In the vicinity of the theater where the ceremony was held platforms had been erected, along which the stars paraded. They arrived in limousines which resembled hearses, in the dizzying glare of the revolving floodlights. On all sides a delirious crowd was roaring and shouting and clapping with hands and feet. Giulietta had seat number thirteen, Anthony Quinn, Dino De Laurentiis and I the following ones. Seated near us were Liz Taylor and Mike Todd, Gary Cooper, Bing Crosby, Frank Sinatra, Cary Grant, James Stewart, Deborah Kerr, Clark Gable, Van Johnson, Janet Gaynor and Alan Ladd. Liz Taylor flaunted a regal-looking diadem like Nefertiti. Amid that display of dazzling fashion, Giulietta, who was wearing a white ermine jacket over a tulle frock, looked like some little pauper girl who had turned up by accident. Many believed that I had plucked her from a circus and dressed her like that for the occasion. Dino De Laurentiis wanted to hand back the Oscar because he had never had faith in the film and hadn't wanted to make it. After the ceremony, we had dinner in a restaurant called Romanov II, where Elsa Maxwell and Louella Parsons held court, tearing those present to pieces without the slightest regard for them. The restaurant was decorated with black velvet; it had the air of a funeral.

So was the ceremony itself something of a funeral?
A vaguely funereal fashion parade, a ceremony in many ways

Fellini on the set of La Strada.

like a carnival, but at the same time a moving and pathetic spectacle, organized with the fullest awareness of what it was and is. Notwithstanding the clamor it excites, it is a private ceremony; it's cinema encountering itself in an attempt to resuscitate the dead, to exorcise wrinkles, old age, illness and death. It has the same fascination as caricature; it is a caricature of the Day of Judgment, the Resurrection of the Flesh. Those like me who accept the mythology of the cinema cannot refuse a prize like the Oscar. To dispute the award seems to me ridiculous and childish. The cinema is also circus, carnival, funfair, a game for acrobats.

Did you expect a second Oscar would come so soon afterward for The Nights of Cabiria?
Absolutely not. The news arrived completely out of the blue and caught us so unawares that we didn't know who should go to pick up the Oscar. Giulietta went. She and I received a rare plaudit for the film. Henry Miller wrote us a letter. He

told us he had seen *The Nights of Cabiria* for the second time in three days and was overcome by tears in front of his friends for ten minutes after the film ended.

The True History of *Rome, Open City*

The story of how Fellini came to be asked to participate in the screenplay for *Rome, Open City* is also told in different versions. Enrico De Seta says: "As far as I'm aware, Rossellini had already shot a short feature on the death of Don Morosini, with Aldo Fabrizi, but afterward decided to do a full-length version. Then Fabrizi said to him, 'I know a young lad, very wet behind the ears, but with phenomenal talent. He's called Federico Fellini. Why not ask him to work on the script?' That's how Rossellini called Fellini."

But everything's a little controversial as regards *Rome, Open City*. The genesis of that memorable film has been described in all its details by the scriptwriter and author Ugo Pirro in *Celluloide*, published by Rizzoli in 1983. Pirro writes:

For the role of Don Morosini, Rossellini and Amidei wanted Fabrizi, but they feared that he would ask for too high a fee. At the time Fabrizi was performing at the Salone Margherita and one evening they went to catch him at the end of the show. Amidei described to him in harrowing detail the part he would play. When he finished Fabrizi had tears in his eyes. "Now he'll do the part for nothing," Rossellini and Amidei thought, exchanging a furtive look of understanding. "I want a million lire," Fabrizi replied, astounding Rossellini and Amidei, for whom such a sum was exorbitant. So Rossellini asked for help from Fellini, who was a great friend of the actor. Fellini, who was by then already a great persuader, convinced him to take the part for 400,000 lire, a sum gradually reduced to 10,000 lire per session, and eventually to a few thousand lire.

Rossellini shot the film not only without money, but also without anything: no technical resources, no crew, not even props. The director had this to say about it:

> I shot the film with very little money picked up with difficulty here and there, a bit at a time; there was scarcely enough to pay for the film, which I couldn't have developed anyway as I wouldn't have had the wherewithal to pay the lab. So we couldn't look at any of the takes until production finished. Later on, having found a little more money, I edited the film and presented it to a limited audience of experts, critics and friends. For almost all of them it was a disappointment.

Rome, Open City was first shown in public in September 1945, at the Teatro Quirino in Rome, but its reception was not much better. Ugo Pirro writes:

> For that evening's scheduled film the audience had only a vague curiosity and a secret hope of witnessing a disastrous flop. The same old anti-Fascist intellectuals had come, sure in the expectation of seeing a farrago which exploited the events of the Nazi occupation for the usual commercial ends. The film had a respectful, but chilly reception. Those who were moved tried to hide the fact. When the word *fine* appeared at the end, there was decorous applause, while everyone wanted the darkness to descend in the auditorium so that they might sneak off without being seen, without having to express judgments and appreciations.

Critical opinion was on the whole negative. The same morning that the notices appeared in the papers, at about nine o'clock, Rossellini telephoned Magnani to read them to her.

"Who's bothering me at this hour?" asked the actress.

"It's me, Roberto. I want to read you the reviews," Rossellini replied.

"I've already read them and sentenced a couple of critics to death," she told him. Then she asked him: "But what time is it?"

"Nine o'clock," he answered.

"O Robé, just because it's you, I'll ask you very nicely to fuck off."

Rossellini started to laugh.

"And why are you laughing, asshole?" Magnani asked him.

"I'm laughing because we've made a great film," Rossellini replied.

"Let's make another one. I want to make another film with you, because although you're a big asshole, you understood everything. Now let me sleep, let's talk about it this evening," she said, hanging up the phone and turning over to sleep.

Concerning Fellini's contribution to *Rome, Open City,* Ugo Pirro writes:

Fellini's contribution was mainly concerned with the dialogue. He suggested many of the gags that allowed Fabrizi to render more manageable the dramatic commitment required to play the role of Don Morosini. He tried to relieve some of the grimness of the plot. The scene in which Don Morosini wallops the sick old man on the head with a frying pan so as to make the man believe he was mortally wounded and in need of extreme unction, thereby justifying his presence in the building, which the suspicious Germans were searching—it was Fellini who thought of it. Fellini had little interest in the rest of the film, whereas his liking for Rossellini grew all the time. Already at that time the images he conjured up were altogether different from those of Rossellini: they began to come to him from the world of the curtain-raiser, to which he was attached by a melancholy affection.

Rossellini, Magnani and Bergman

In February 1981 Fellini asked me to dinner at his house at 110 Via Margutta, the Roman street where artists lived. After dinner he indulged in memories of the heroic postwar period, recounting among other things the flight of Roberto Rossellini to America to meet Ingrid Bergman and the reaction of Anna Magnani. It was 1948. Rossellini had received Bergman's famous letter: "Dear Mister Rossellini, I have seen *Rome, Open City* and *Paisà* and enjoyed them immensely. If you require a Swedish actress who speaks very good English, has not forgotten her German, hardly understands French and in Italian can only say "I love you," I am ready to come to Italy to work with you." But instead the director decided to go to America himself.

At that time Rossellini and Anna Magnani were staying at the Excelsior, the most elegant hotel on the Via Veneto. The actress had stipulated that her three dogs must also be lodged in their suite. One morning the director got up as quietly as possible, tiptoed into the bathroom, got dressed without making the slightest noise and made his way to the front door.

"Robé, where are you going?" the actress asked him, waking up unexpectedly just as he got to the door.

"I'm taking the dogs for a walk to the Villa Borghese," the director replied, searching for a plausible excuse.

"At this hour? It's dawn."

"I'm a bit on edge, I couldn't sleep."

"OK then, take the dogs to the Villa Borghese."

So he was obliged to take the dogs out with him. But as soon as he got to the lobby he entrusted them to the doorman, had him call a cab and sped to Fiumicino to catch his flight to America.

The actress turned the whole hotel upside down. She even took it out on the dogs, accusing them of not having made the slightest sign to let her know that Rossellini was about to pull a fast one on her. She heaped ferocious abuse on them: "Stupid beasts! Filthy scoundrels! Lousy traitors!"

While Fellini was telling the story, Giulietta Masina occasionally shook her head. At the end of it she said to him, "You told that story very well, but you forgot to mention one thing."

"What have I forgotten to say, Giulietta?"

"The most important thing."

"What's that?"

"That Roberto didn't behave like a gentleman."

"But how does that come into it, Giulietta?"

"Of course it does, and how!"

"No, Giulietta."

"You ought to have said . . ."

"What ought I to have said?"

"That Roberto behaved like a bastard!"

"Giulietta, I was only telling a story."

"If you didn't say that Roberto behaved like a bastard, then you must have approved of his behavior."

"I'm not approving of anything, Giulietta."

"If you won't say that he behaved like a bastard, it means that you are his accomplice."

"But what have I got to do with it, Giulietta?"

"Why won't you say that he behaved like a bastard?"

"Please, Giulietta."

"I know why you won't say it."

"Why do I not say it?"

"Because you would have behaved like him."

"Giulietta and I are the perfect Italian couple," Fellini said, gently caressing his wife as he got up to see us to the door.

Fellini and Flaiano

Fellini and Flaiano began to work together in 1949–50 on *Variety Lights,* the film directed by Alberto Lattuada and the aspiring director from Rimini. Flaiano, who arrived in Rome in 1922 from his native Pescara, was forty. He was a film and theater critic, scriptwriter, journalist, playwright and novelist. In 1945 he wrote a play, *The War Explained to the Poor,* which was performed in 1946 at the Arlecchino Theater in Rome. In 1947 he published a novel, *Time to Kill,* which in the same year won the Strega, a new but important literary prize.

But the collaboration between Fellini and Flaiano, the former as director and the latter as scriptwriter or coscriptwriter, began officially in 1951–52 with *The White Sheikh* and lasted for thirteen years, until *Juliet of the Spirits.* Starting with *Toby Dammit,* Bernardino Zapponi took over from Fellini's regular scriptwriters, Flaiano, Tullio Pinelli and Brunello Rondi. He went on to write, in collaboration with the director, *A Director's Notebook, Satyricon, The Clowns, Roma, Fellini's Casanova* and *City of Women.*

It wasn't long before the working and social relations between Fellini and Flaiano were disturbed by misunderstandings, incomprehensions, petulance, recriminations and resentment. It was Flaiano above all who lamented the affronts, real or imagined, that he received from Fellini. Fellini made every effort to reassure and placate him, but it was a difficult task. And since they couldn't manage to patch up their differences face to face, they would write each other letters.

In a letter dated April 24, 1955, Flaiano accused Fellini of holding a press conference on *Il Bidone* without telling him or Tullio Pinelli. "You wanted to be solely responsible," he wrote, "for a story which is not yet a film, but merely a script, passing over the fact that it was I and Pinelli alone who wrote the screenplay, who have created it bit by bit over five months of hard work, and who were worried in a brotherly way lest you abandon the idea of doing a film. All forgotten? Fine. On other occasions, always at the end of some common endeavor, your behavior has been less than loyal in comparison to ours." It was the official opening of hostilities. In an undated letter, Fellini replied by sending his regards, and in a Christmas letter in 1957 he wrote to Flaiano: "Every time I feel lost and absentminded, I'm reminded painfully of you."

But the crucial year for their relationship was 1964. In the spring the journalist Sergio Saviano wrote in *L'Espresso* that the association between Fellini and his screenwriters Flaiano, Pinelli and Rondi, was over. On June 7 Flaiano wrote a letter to Fellini in which he confirms the end of their collaboration, adding: "We hope that while you're working on the film *[Juliet of the Spirits]* you think up some good dialogue. Our name is at stake."

In the course of the same year two incidents occurred that stretched to the limit the tension between them.

8½ was nominated for an Oscar. Fellini, Masina, Flaiano and the other scriptwriters left for Los Angeles. Angelo Rizzoli, the producer of the film, paid for the tickets: first class for the director and his wife, but only second class for the scriptwriters. When they arrived in New York, Flaiano bought himself a first-class ticket with his own money and promptly flew back to Rome. Flaiano's friends said, "It is true that it was Angelo Rizzoli who booked the tickets, but Fellini could have made efforts to ensure that everyone was in first class, or at least, if it came to it, once they were on the plane, could have transferred to second class."

The second incident was altogether more serious. At that time Fellini was careful to sing Flaiano's praises, but, between one compliment and another, he let slip the following comment: "Flaiano made no material or technical contribution to the drawing up of the screenplay, but his jokes were very valuable." Perhaps Fellini exaggerated. Others state that Flaiano participated fully in the screenplay, writing dialogue and other parts of the script and not limiting himself merely to making up jokes.

Fellini and Flaiano rarely saw each other again, although they continued to write to each other. On October 23, 1969 Flaiano wrote Fellini a letter in which he paid him rather ambiguous compliments for *Satyricon*. One of Fellini's last letters is dated March 5, 1972, nine months before the writer died. Fellini had said that it was a pity that Flaiano wasn't wholly identified with his proper vocation as a writer, and Flaiano was offended. In the letter Fellini made a last, vain attempt at reconciliation.

The truth is that Flaiano was a very touchy man. Although very witty when dealing with other people, he couldn't extend the same sense of humor toward himself. His closest friends confirmed this fact, including the journalist Giulia Massari and the painter Mino Maccari. At the beginning of December 1960 Vittorio Gassman staged Flaiano's best-known comedy, *A Martian in Rome,* at the Lorico Theater in Milan. Massari, who was present, with Maccari, recounts: "The show was a resounding flop. The theater erupted, as they say, but in whistles, not applause. Flaiano was desperate. He wandered about the theater like a madman, rebuking Gassman. Then Maccari said, 'The unsuccess has gone to his head.' "

Maccari for his part related: "Flaiano and I had been like brothers for many years. And yet for that remark he turned his back on me and didn't speak to me for a year. The ability to laugh at oneself is a rare gift. Not even Flaiano had it. Massari adds: "Since I was reduced to laughter by Maccari's witticism, Flaiano ever after behaved coldly toward me."

But the real reason that Fellini and Flaiano practically broke off relations is deeper. Flaiano nurtured an acute frustration within himself, not only because the glory of the films he had worked on with Fellini was enjoyed chiefly by the director, but also because he would have liked to have worked as a director himself. He had tried to turn one of his own stories, *Melampo,* into a film, but didn't succeed. (It was later used for the film *La Cagna* by Mario Ferreri). Paul Mazursky told me in 1993 in Los Angeles, "Flaiano felt frustrated in comparison with Fellini because he didn't succeed in becoming a film director."

Fellini and Pasolini

Fellini and Pasolini met each other in the fifties, much earlier than their encounter at Cineriz. When Fellini was preparing *The Nights of Cabiria*, Pasolini had accompanied him on a car trip through Rome in search of "la Bomba," the archetypal prostitute of the Roman suburbs, and he had afterward participated in the screenplay of that film. Meantime Pasolini had written an account of that trip including a long and detailed portrait of Fellini. This account was published in the monograph on *The Nights of Cabiria*, and Pasolini recalled it in one of his poems, *The Religion of My Time* (1957–59). In 1992 it was republished in the volume *The Rules of an Illusion* and by the weekly *L'Espresso* as if it had never been published before. It is an extraordinary portrait:

> I'll always remember the morning I met Fellini: a "fabulous" morning, to use his favorite epithet. We set off from the Piazza del Popolo in his car, which was as big and soft, giddy and yet controlled as he was. Eventually we reached the country-side: was it Flaminia? Aurelia? Cassia? Fellini drove with one hand, glancing here and there at the scenery, constantly at risk of running over a child or ending up in the ditch, but somehow giving the impression that such a thing was inconceivable. He drove the car by magic, as if controlling it by a thread. So, with his one hand gripping the steering wheel (with the desperate motherliness of a middle-aged woman and the fervid concentration of an alchemist), and the other playing with his hair, using his forefinger as a lathe or spindle, I was carried through a countryside bathed in the soft hon-eyed light of the season while he told me the plot of *Nights of Cabiria*. I, a little Peruvian cat beside a big Siamese, lis-tened with Auerbach in my pocket.
>
> I still didn't understand Fellini. I thought I could identify, by limited qualities, what I later realized was a far greater talent. Imagine a great slug as big as a city—Knossos or

Palmyra—which you enter like a Rabelaisian hero. Inside you come across things which disappoint you initially, like a gas station or a little whore walking the streets. There's a sense of discrepancy between the vastness of the setting and the meanness of the objects found there. But a little later you realize that the labyrinth slug digests and assimilates everything—horrendous and radiant—in its viscera, even you, if you're not careful.

The shape of Fellini's body is rather protean. It tends to reorganize itself and settle into the next shape that suggests itself. A huge mass of flesh which according to its imagination can resemble an octopus, an amoeba magnified under a microscope, an Aztec ruin, a drowned cat. But all it takes is a gust of wind, a swerve of the car, to mix everything up again, and turn the organism into a man again, a very gentle, intelligent, sly and alarmed man, with two ears created in the most advanced acoustic laboratory. And a mouth which scatters about the strangest phonemes that a hybrid Rimini-Rome dialect has ever produced—shouts, exclamations, interjections, diminutives—the whole battery of rural preliteralism.

When he referred to *The Nights of Cabiria,* I became apprehensive of the disproportion between the concrete nature of the tone, environment and flavor of the film, and the almost surreal nature of its imaginative origin, redeemed as it is by humor. I made notes and told him all this in the evening, still ensconced in his car, parked under a light on a risky side street just where we could land the sought-after *battona,* la Bomba. He listened to me slumped down on the old leather seat like a broody hen, a cloaked Madonna, with his jowly face. His eyes betrayed fixed concentration or anxiety. Perhaps he was a little alarmed by my Auerbach.

We never found la Bomba, although we scoured all the alleyways that snaked around the Passeggiata Archeologica with their knots of red prostitutes lit up by stabbing headlights and thugs in gangs or alone, sitting astride walls, with their pert little backsides and their jacket collars turned up gracefully about their heads, which were adorned, like a wedding cake, with a straight white part between tight curls.

L'Espresso asked Fellini to give his account of this trip with Pasolini. Another extraordinary description:

I telephoned him after I had read *Ragazzi di Vita* to express my admiration; he was very nice and spoke in flattering terms about *Vitelloni* and *La Strada*. A little later, when the script of *The Nights of Cabiria* was ready, I thought about asking him to read it for his opinion on how to deal with the slang. Our appointment was at the bar Canova in Piazza del Popolo. I saw him come in and he struck me at once as very likable, all covered in dust like a bricklayer. He had a proletarian appearance, like a bantamweight, or a street fighter. He accepted my proposal of working with me with enthusiasm. He was a generous and impulsive man and we set off on that car ride, which he describes so well. It's true that we were both a bit like slugs, and he had something greedy in his eyes, an inexhaustible curiosity. I drove with him through certain parts of the city that were sunk in ominous silence, hellish slum areas with suggestive names, Infernetto, Tiburtino III, Cessati Spiriti. He guided me as if he were Virgil and Charon combined; he had the look of both, but also the look of a sheriff, a little sheriff checking up on familiar areas. He was amused by my alarm, smiling the smile of someone who has seen a lot worse and in fact wishing that something worse would happen to amuse his friend. Every so often dark figures would pop out from windows, doors and corners, street boys that he delighted in introducing to me as if we were in the Amazon among fantastic, wild, ancient beings. He seemed to me, in the short time I knew him, someone drunk on the implicit danger of his diabolic, anonymous persona. In his last years he wore dark glasses and dressed like a hero in a science fantasy film, like *Terminator,* with a leather jacket. By then he had become more silent and tended toward immobility.

In the same article Fellini also recalled how Federiz was set up and the incident with Pasolini:

Federiz—the "z" stood for Rizzoli and "Federi" for Federico —hoped to help young directors make their first film. In reality all that I succeeded in doing for the company was to find an office and furnish it. I amused myself for months turning it into an old convent or into the tavern of the Three Musketeers. For ten months I played host to the jobless of Cinecittà. Nearby, in Via della Croce, was the Cesaretto restaurant and at one o'clock it was an easy matter to have some food brought over; the place looked like a canteen. But in the early months, our enthusiasm was considerable and even I was convinced that we were going to produce certain fine films made by other directors: *El Cochecito* by Marco Ferreri, *Il Posto* by Ermanno Olmi and Pasolini's *Accattone.* Pier Paolo was confident of his abilities as a director. The script was wonderful and he asked if he could do some screen tests. We had to overcome the resistance of Rizzoli and the other partner, Clemente Fracassi, who was very shrewd but prone to pessimism regarding the finances. As for me, I was still playing the producer and was irresponsible rather than optimistic. Pier Paolo shot the screen tests and, swayed by the unfavorable opinions of Rizzoli and Fracassi as well as an overly personal view of things, I made a judgment, a mistaken one. I was forced to tell Pier Paolo not the truth, but that it was better to wait. Intelligent as he was, he understood that I was also unwilling to proceed, which wasn't true. Smiling with a little sadness he said to me, "Of course I can't make films the way you do."

The incident at Cineriz damaged beyond repair relations between Fellini and Pasolini. In the interview which he gave to *L'Espresso* in which he recalled the screen tests which Pasolini made, Fellini toned down the incident considerably. By then many years had passed: Pasolini had died in 1975; worse, in the most gruesome of circumstances. What purpose could be served by telling the whole truth? But the truth indeed was very different. Enrico De Seta recounts: "After *La Dolce Vita,* I called on Fellini at Cineriz. He told me that, among the other aspiring directors, that little shit Pasolini had also been present, who gave himself such great literary airs." To others also, Fellini had said that the screen tests were a disaster. As Moraldo Rossi, who in those years was one of his colleagues as well as one of his closest friends, relates:

Fellini said to me, with an apparently sad air, "I don't know what to do with Pasolini. He's brought me stuff that even the worst news cameraman would not dare show me. And to think he talks of Dreyer." At that time I often met Pasolini in the evening. He was so depressed, so desperate as to make me fear that he would kill himself. He had staked everything on Fellini, but Fellini had dropped him. Subsequently, when he had begun to shoot *Accattone* with the producer Alfredo Bini, Pasolini quoted me the title of the Truman Capote novel, *Other Voices, Other Rooms.* He was trying to say that between himself and Fellini there was no possibility of mutual understanding. Theirs were indeed two separate worlds. Later Fellini recognized that Pasolini was a writer, but still without great conviction. As for Pasolini, he always talked of Fellini with great wariness.

Concerning Pasolini's contribution to *The Nights of Cabiria,* Moraldo Rossi writes:

Fellini had asked Pasolini to write some of the screenplay. Pasolini brought him about forty pages. Fellini glanced over them and passed them on to me, without using them at all. I've still got those pages. Maybe Fellini did use some slang expressions and some advice as to the gestures to accompany certain slang words. When we came to shoot the film, Fellini regarded Pasolini as extraneous. I remember that we shot some scenes at Acilia, between Rome and Ostia. Pasolini was seated all alone on a rock, wearing a T-shirt and eating a sandwich. Fellini said, "All he needs is a feather in his head to look like a Red Indian." Besides, in those years Fellini had a complete aversion to homosexuals. One day, he, Pasolini and myself met near Piazza del Popolo. We talked about women and about love. Bidding us farewell, Pasolini said, "I tell you that the most beautiful thing in the world is making love." Fellini commented, "But what's this crap he's saying? He talks of love but for him that means taking it up the ass." Subsequently Fellini altered his attitude toward homosexuals. The cinema world was full of them and we had to secure many of them for *La Dolce Vita*.

La Dolce Vita, Anita Ekberg, Marcello Mastroianni

COSTANZO COSTANTINI: *What in particular do you now remember about* La Dolce Vita?
FEDERICO FELLINI: For me the film is identified more with Anita Ekberg than with the Via Veneto.

What was she like? What impression did she make when you met her for the first time?
She possessed incredible beauty. I first met her toward the end of 1959 in the Hotel de la Ville, the hotel in the center of Rome where she was staying. I had never seen anyone like her; she made a great impression on me. Later the same day I met Marcello Mastroianni, who later told me that Ekberg reminded him of a storm trooper in the *Wehrmacht,* but really he didn't want to admit that even he had never before seen such marvelous and unbelievable beauty.

How did that first encounter go?
She wanted to see the script, to know who the other actresses were and what her character was like.

Ekberg says that she asked you, "Where's the script?" and that you replied, "There isn't one." True?
More or less.

And then she said to her agent, "I told you this was a joke. This man isn't a director, he's a madman. How can you make a film without a script?"
She was with her agent, but I don't remember if she said to him what she now remembers saying. I don't believe that she would have said that I was a madman in front of me.

Is it true you said to her, "I'll explain to you what you have to do, then we'll write the script; better still, you write the script"?
I don't remember; it was so long ago.

Is it true she said to her agent, "But is this man really a director? He wants me to write the script. I've never written anything, except for letters to my mother in Sweden. He doesn't want me to have a part in his film—but maybe he's after something else from me"?
How do I know what she said to her agent? I remember that a few days later I sent her some little slips of paper explaining what she had to do and afterward we started shooting. As I did with the rest of the cast, day by day I would write out the lines she had to say and then ask her, "You like them? If not, we'll change them."

Ekberg immersed herself in the Trevi Fountain without difficulty?
Ekberg came from the North, she was young and as proud of her good health as a lioness. She was no trouble at all. She remained immersed in the basin for ages, motionless, impassive, as if the water didn't cover her nor the cold affect her, even though it was March and the nights made one shiver. For Mastroianni it was a rather different story. He had to get

undressed, put on a frogman's suit and get dressed again. To combat the cold he polished off a bottle of vodka, and when we shot the scene he was completely pissed.

How long did you take to shoot that scene?
It took eight or nine nights. Some of the owners of the surrounding houses would rent out their balconies and windows to the curious. At the end of each take the crowd would cheer. A show within a show. Every time I look at the picture of Ekberg in the Trevi Fountain, I have the sensation of reliving those magic moments, those sleepless nights, surrounded by the meowing of cats and the crowd that gathered from every corner of the city.

Is it true that when you first met Mastroianni in Fregene, you said to him, "I thought of you for the part of the protagonist because you have such an ordinary face"? It's what Mastroianni himself has said.
First of all I have to say that wasn't the first time I saw him. He doesn't remember it, but I first met him in 1948, at the Theater of the Arts, where he was appearing with Giulietta in *Angelica* by Leo Ferrero. Giulietta introduced him to me after the show, when I went with her to his dressing room to give my compliments. Later he sent me a telegram for *Vitelloni*, saying how much he had enjoyed the film. Giulietta often mentioned him and when I began preparing *La Dolce Vita* suggested him to me for the part of the journalist. I don't remember if I had seen any of the films he had made previously, but, in direct opposition to the wishes of Dino De Laurentiis, who wanted Paul Newman at all costs, I asked him over to Fregene; it was noon. I was at the Villa dei Pini with Flaiano. He came; we chatted a bit, in rather vague terms. But I don't think I said to him, "I thought of you because you have an ordinary face." It's not the sort of thing I'd say.

What did you say to him?
I gave him the outline of the role: a somewhat cynical journalist, a witness, but at the same time implicated in what he witnesses. I don't think I treated him condescendingly, seated as I was and he standing. I hadn't the slightest desire to humiliate him. Probably I said something to him to explain my reasons for rejecting Paul Newman. How could Paul Newman be believable as a journalist in Via Veneto, when he himself would have been the object of the chasing pack of paparazzi? What was required was an actor who wasn't a household name. I remember De Laurentiis saying to me, "He's too soft and goody-goody; a family man rather than the type who flings women onto the bed." As an alternative to Paul Newman he suggested Gérard Philipe, but that came to nothing and he ended up giving up the film.

Mastroianni has said that when he asked you for the script, you said to Flaiano, "Ennio, give it to him," and Flaiano passed you a piece of card which had only a rather obscene drawing on it.
We change our accounts of events continually so as not to bore ourselves. But the story of the drawing is true. It showed a man with a huge penis floating on his back and stealing a peep at the half-naked women all around him. Marcello was disconcerted by it, thinking we wanted to pull his leg. But it wasn't so. Ennio and I were always joking. I said we would see each other again, and in fact we met up in Rome a few days later. We drove around Rome and a good rapport developed between us, so I decided to engage him. Peppino Amato, the producer and director who had produced Rossellini's *The Flowers of Saint Francis,* took over from De Laurentiis. Everyone tried to make a deal in advance, as has always been the case ever since, and by the time it fell into the lap of Angelo Rizzoli, the film had cost a fortune.

Is it true that when the film was screened for a gala evening at the Capitol in Milan on February 5, 1960, an infuriated member of the audience spat in your face?
Marcello and I only just saved ourselves from a lynching. I was spat at in the face and he received insults like "layabout," "scoundrel," "debauchee," "communist." The *Osservatore Romano* retitled the film *The Disgusting Life.* Some went so far as to demand that it be burned and I be deprived of my passport. In truth, Italian critics were very favorable, but it was abroad that it enjoyed widespread and immediate approval. The evening of its official screening at Cannes was memorable. Anita, Marcello and I along with the rest of the cast walked back to the hotel, flanked by a delirious crowd. Georges Simenon and Henry Miller, president and member of the International Jury respectively, had fought for the film to be awarded the Palme d'Or.

La Dolce Vita *marked a decisive close to a great period of Italian cinema: neorealism. What is your judgment on neorealism now?*
I'd prefer to say the film represented a development rather than a closing of the movement. I have already said that I identify neorealism primarily with Roberto Rossellini. The other father of neorealism was Cesare Zavattini. He is a poet, a copious source of ideas, invention and new perspectives. The collaboration between Zavattini and Vittorio De Sica yielded much fruit: *Sciuscià, Bicycle Thieves, Umberto D., Miracle in Milan.* If I remember correctly, *Miracle in Milan* appeared in the same year as Rossellini's *The Flowers of Saint Francis,* which represented a decisive stage in the development of neorealism. Up until then the movement had been a spontaneous impulse to view reality with disenchanted and liberated eyes, a way of taking stock of the contemporary world. Now what was needed was knowledge of humanity, by turning those same eyes upon the inner man. *The Flowers of Saint Francis* was a step in this

direction, leading the way for Rossellini's later films, culminating with *General Della Rovere*. Neorealism pretended to derive directly from life, but life transforms itself incessantly. Rossellini had the sensitivity always to keep in tune with the shifting wavelength of real life, even if it meant contradicting his theoretical principles. But neorealism was exploited somewhat excessively, even for purely commercial reasons. If there hadn't been this exploitation, we would all call ourselves neorealists today.

Anita Ekberg's Version

It is amusing to hear Anita Ekberg's account of her performance in *La Dolce Vita* and of the sequence where she plunges herself into the Trevi Fountain:

> Ever since I was a little girl I dreamed that one day I would go to Rome. I went there for the first time in 1955, to act in *War and Peace,* directed by King Vidor. I stayed at the Hotel de la Ville, near Trinità dei Monti. At that time there wasn't the chaos that there is now and from the hotel to Cinecittà took only five minutes. I drove a Mercedes 300SL convertible with the top always down, even when it rained, my hair blowing in the wind. Probably Fellini noticed me passing in the street or at Cinecittà.
>
> When we were shooting, each day Fellini would write some lines and then ask me, "What do you think of them? If you don't like them we'll change them." We came to the scene in the Trevi Fountain. That scene had already happened in reality, before Fellini thought it up. One night I was having photos taken by the film's photographer Luigi. I was barefoot and I cut my foot. I went in search of a fountain to bathe my bleeding foot and, all unawares, found myself in the Piazza di Trevi. It was summer. I was wearing a white-and-pink cotton dress with the upper part like a man's shirt. I lifted the skirt up and

Masters of Italian cinema: De Sica, Rossellini and Fellini.

immersed myself in the basin, saying to Luigi, "You can't imagine how cool this water is; you should come in, too." "Just stay like that," he said and started taking photos. They sold like hotcakes. But the difference was that I took the plunge in August, whereas Fellini made me do it in March. It was I who made Fellini famous, not the other way around. When the film was presented in New York, the distributor reproduced the fountain scene on a billboard as high as a skyscraper. My name was in the middle in huge letters, Fellini's was at the bottom, very tiny. Now the name Fellini has become very great, mine very little. Everyone said I didn't have any talent, only long blond hair and a marvelous bust, but *La Dolce Vita* was a piece of cake for me; I could have done it blindfolded. They're always showing that scene again on television. The commentators never say "Fellini's *Dolce Vita* with Anita Ekberg," but "Anita Ekberg's *Dolce Vita* with Fellini," or simply "*La Dolce Vita* with Anita Ekberg."

La Dolce Vita caused an unprecedented scandal. Fellini was accused of having made Rome into a symbol of human folly, vice and perdition. Evelyn Waugh proclaimed that Rome was threatened by a new barbarian invasion and that he knew of no other city in the world where one breathed an atmosphere of such irremediable decadence.

As Fellini recalled, the Rome *Osservatore,* organ of the Vatican, wrote no fewer than seven pieces against the film, each more ferocious than the last. But the Jesuits did not hesitate to come to the defense of the film, in defiance of the wrath of the Vatican.

Angelo Arpa, the father of the Society of Jesus who had been a friend of Fellini's since the fifties, recounts:

> I showed *La Dolce Vita* first in the San Fedele Centre in Milan and afterward in the Arecco Institute in Genoa. Reactions among those present in Milan were favorable, but in the Vatican things were even worse than before. The director of

Mastroianni and Ekberg at the Trevi Fountain.

the San Fedele Centre, Father Nazareno Taddei, was dismissed, while I was severely reprimanded by the highest authorities. Cardinal Siri, president of the Italian Episcopal Conference and a source of real power in the Vatican, himself attended the screening in Genoa. Afterward he asked me what I thought of it. "From the point of view of the language, it's a new and original film." "And from the moral point of view?" he asked. "It's a film that makes one think," I replied. "I'll show it to my seminarists," he concluded. Subsequently he wrote a very nice letter to Fellini. But even the opinion of Cardinal Siri counted for nothing in the Vatican. After the articles in the *Osservatore* the film was forbidden to Catholics, who saw it on pain of excommunication. I asked the editor of the *Osservatore,* Count Giuseppe Della Torre, "But have you seen the film?" "I don't need to see that filth," he replied.

Only in 1994, after Fellini's death, was *La Dolce Vita* rehabilitated. In an article that appeared in *Civiltà Catholica,* the journal of the Society of Jesus, Father Virgilio Fantuzzi wrote:

If Fellini's earlier films can be compared to so many *viae crucis* travelled by those carrying what Pier Paolo Pasolini called "filthy crucifixes without thorns," so too can *La Dolce Vita* in its own fashion: in it we can contemplate the stages along the *via doloroso* of a sinner who reflects upon his own inadequacy when confronted by the obligations that life thrusts upon him.

8½, *Juliet of the Spirits*, Fregene, *Fellini Satyricon*, *The Clowns*

COSTANZO COSTANTINI: *When you were planning* 8½, *you said that the film would not present particular problems of interpretation. However, for the majority of the public the film proved incomprehensible. In Cosenza in Calabria, the spectators tried to attack the projectionist in protest against the obscurity of the film.*
FEDERICO FELLINI: I'm not a good judge of my films and I don't want to be. making films is my way of life: when I'm not shooting a film, I'm preparing one. But it doesn't seem to me that *8½* is a difficult film to understand. For me it was a liberating experience and I hope it also liberates the viewers, even if it didn't work for the audiences in Cosenza.

But you're satisfied with the film, with your colleagues and cast?
Yes; why not? By now I've reached a perfect rapport with my production team. I feel toward the cast the same sense of tenderness and affection that the puppeteer has for his puppets. Cinema uses the close-up, which is a pitiless X ray of what's inside you. The miracle consists in allowing the authenticity to shine through the artifice. Mastroianni has shown the most humble and total sensitivity: his exceptional performance is the result of this. Anouk Aimée makes one forget the dark and sensual personage of *La Dolce Vita*. Claudia Cardinale was as important for me as the fairy with deep blue hair was for Pi-

nocchio. Sandra Milo is delightful. The rest of the cast are all wonderful. As far as I'm concerned, I can say that *8½* seems to me a film sincere to the point of being indecent, perhaps irritating. It's also a comic and amusing film.

For no other of your films have the critics raked up so many possible influences: Kierkegaard, Proust, Gide, Joyce, Bergman, Resnais, Pirandello.
I work in such an isolated state that I don't give a thought to critical opinion. It's extraneous to the germination of my ideas and to their cinematographic realization. Afterward, when the film is finished, I'm pleased with favorable criticism, on a rather petty level; in contrast, negative criticism makes me instinctively defensive. In the case of *8½,* I sensed on the part of the critics a solidarity that went beyond their profession, beyond aesthetic fact.

Critics have mentioned Last Year at Marienbad *by Resnais. What do you think of this comparison?*
I haven't seen Resnais's film. I've only seen some stills and read some reviews. It's clear to me that the film operates on the level of pure intellectual abstraction. In this respect, *8½* is the complete antithesis. What I'm saying is awkward, but it's true. If a man is receptive to life, he is also receptive to certain cultural facts; certain issues are in the air, and they can be grasped intuitively.

In fact, while you were making 8½, *Ingmar Bergman was making* The Silence, *Arthur Miller was writing* After the Fall, *Elia Kazan* The Anatolian Smile, *Jean-Paul Sartre* Words, *Max Frisch* Gantenbein—*all works of a subjective and autobiographical nature.*
But I have nothing to do with these works.

8½: Fellini on set.

Have you not read Joyce's Ulysses? *According to Alberto Moravia, you must have read it and thought about it: Guido Anselmi, the protagonist of the film, resembles Leopold Bloom.*

I'm sorry to disappoint Moravia, but I haven't read *Ulysses.*

Other critics have cited Kierkegaard, Guido Gozzano, Marino Moretti. Do you find these suggestions relevant?

In one way such comparisons flatter me, because they put me in the company of respectable writers; in another they sadden

8½: The circus ring.

me, because literary references are not necessary to understand my films. The critics who got nearest to the meaning of *8½* were those who didn't look for any influences. On the other hand, I can't comment on the pertinence of such cited influences because I don't know the authors to whom they refer. Kierkegaard and Marino Moretti I know by name; I may have read some of Gozzano's poetry at school. I don't wish to defend my ignorance in this way. There are so many books I plan to read, but I never find the time. Anyway, life interests me much more than books. Museums and libraries are not made for artists. It's true that in reading certain books one encounters useful and extraordinary things, one communes with great spirits; but I am a casual and unsystematic reader. I'm not well-informed.

Have you read Proust, the author most mentioned in relation to 8½?
I'm sorry, but I'm afraid I must say I haven't.

You've seen Wild Strawberries? *It's also been mentioned in connection with 8½.*
It was enough to see this film for me to realize what a great artist Bergman is. But I had *8½* in mind for about six years; that's even before I started thinking about *La Dolce Vita*. However, it is a comparison that flatters me. Bergman is a real showman, who uses everything, even illusionism, an esoteric illusionism which presents in a playful manner a problematic and disturbing reality. He's not a director who loves good taste, nice-looking sets. Bergman and I share the same mutual sympathy: we feel the blood of the human race, which has something of the dust of the circus in its salty tang.

Pardon an indiscreet question: how many films have you seen and how many books have you read in the past five years? And what were they?
Besides *Wild Strawberries* I've seen Kurosawa's *Seven Samurai*. Bergman and Kurosawa are true creators, magicians, but not in the sense of mystification: they have a real, rich world of fantasy and they portray it with force, without refraining from using the tricks of the trade. I've seen Chaplin's *A King in New York*, Pasolini's *Accattone*, Brunello Rondi's *Una Vita Violenta*, Ferreri's *El Cochecito*, Franco Rossi's *Odissea Nuda*. I've read *Tempo di uccidere* by Flaiano and Moravia's *La noia*. Moravia possesses a disconcerting lucidity, but he lacks the ability to yield to the irrational: I think that the constancy with which he defends the power of reason will end up leading him to a kind of mysticism. My favorite writers are Landolfi and Gadda. I'm a passionate reader of magic books, court reports and newspaper items.

Recently you declared that you needed to free yourself from Catholicism. But without it, would you not perhaps be like the cynical intellectual who figures in 8½?
Yes, but at the end of *8½* the protagonist realizes that his fear, complexes and anxiety are in fact a kind of wealth.

Isn't that saying of St. Augustine's—"Love and do what you wish"—altogether too convenient? It can be interpreted in a distorted way to justify any individual caprice.
No, no. I appreciate the equivocations to which a phrase like that can give rise, but St. Augustine means that you need to love first and then you can do anything you want. Love is the most difficult thing in the world. I mean love in the Christian sense, the love that makes one complete, that puts one on a more vital level of great power, but this is the highest peak, the most unattainable.

You won your third Oscar for 8½. How were you received in Los Angeles? You were no longer the almost unknown Fellini of La Strada, *but a world-famous director.*
This time we went to Hollywood in convoy: I, Giulietta, Angelo Rizzoli, Ennio Flaiano, Sandra Milo and the producer Morris Ergas. Piero Gherardi was also with us, the costume designer who had won an Oscar for *La Dolce Vita* and now a second for *8½*. The atmosphere around us really had changed. I remember one night, while I was walking through our hotel, I was stopped by a cop. "I'm Federico Fellini," I told him, but he refused to believe me. Anyway, prior to the Oscar, the film had enjoyed great success in New York, and had received the Grand Prize at the Moscow Festival, where I also attended the presentation. *8½* was given a gala evening at the new festival cinema and a normal screening at the embassy. At the gala were Joan Crawford, Claudette Colbert, Myrna Loy, Shelley Winters, Arthur Miller and Elia Kazan. The American public

had understood *8½* better than the Italian, perhaps because they are more used to psychoanalytic interpretation, even if it's somewhat vague.

Were you tempted to set a film in New York?
New York would be the most congenial city for my films. It's a city that fascinates me; its people are completely mad, but profoundly human. One day there was a wedding in my hotel. Not even the most ferocious caricaturist could have succeeded in doing justice to the participants: 100-year-old women dressed in pink like newborn babies; a man with multicolored hair like a beach umbrella. But cinema is a concrete language, which requires total control over everything. It's not a matter of merely reproducing things as they appear, but of producing them in the first place. Perhaps I'm saying all this because I don't have the courage to tackle a city as abnormal and wild as New York. I prefer to continue making films in Rome or elsewhere in Italy, in the environment I know at Cinecittà, Studio 5, where my friends visit me—directors both Italian and foreign—and gladden me with their affection.

Which directors have visited you at Cinecittà?
I recall a visit of Bergman's, who had also come to shoot a film. I showed him around the place. With us was the director of Cinecittà, Pasqualone Lancia. That day it was raining cats and dogs. Pasqualone had procured an umbrella for himself and was wearing an ankle-length raincoat, which made him look like a priest, like a country curate. Bergman wore a raincoat that was too short for him, the back of his head shaven like a soldier's. Hands behind his back and with the gait of a Kierkegaardian or Beckettian enquirer, he walked on ahead of Pasqualone without listening to what he was mumbling underneath the umbrella. A few meters in front a stray dog eyed us with suspicion.

But which film was Bergman about to shoot there?
I don't remember, but I remember that visit in every detail. The usual gang of out-of-work extras, actors and electricians was gathered in the bar. With a feverish and fixed expression, like a medium in a trance, Bergman didn't notice this little society in their fishermen's raincoats smoking behind the dirty, steamed-up windows. He just shook his head as a sign of refusal when I asked him if he wanted a coffee. In silence we made the tour of the studios, until Bergman asked us unexpectedly where the toilets were. Pasqualone looked at me in dismay. The toilets at Cinecittà were disgusting and the roof leaked; along the dilapidated corridors and through the peeling doors could be heard the hoarse voice of a drunk singing "Birimbo Birimba" behind one of the doors and making disgusting noises. To remedy this disaster, I asked Pasqualone to take us to the swimming pool. Out of the frying pan into the fire: we beheld a wasteland of cement and ruins, like a stage set for *The Fall of the House of Usher.*

In the space of a few minutes you've already mentioned three writers: Kierkegaard, Beckett and Poe. How many others will you refer to before you finish the story?
I'm talking about Bergman and must keep myself on a suitably elevated plane. As the rain started to fall even more heavily, Bergman pointed out to me with his very long finger a corner of the swimming pool. Beneath the rain-rippled surface of the water an infinity of little organisms, like a Sumerian alphabet, were whirling around at bacterial velocity. Bergman squatted down on his heels and began talking to the tadpoles with a happy smile on his face. Pasqualone retired a discreet distance to leave us alone.

What did he say to you when you were alone?
Just at that moment the clouds opened up and the funereal

scene was bathed in yellow light. We turned back in silence, without exchanging a word, not even farewells when we parted.

But were you due to do a film with Bergman?
I was going to do one with him and Kurosawa. All three of us were looking forward to it. We all shared a perfect rapport, and just because of this, nothing came of it, as is the way in Rome.

You've said a number of times that Juliet of the Spirits *was your first color film. But had you not already used color in* The Temptation of Doctor Antonio, *the second episode of* Boccaccio '70, *in which you used Anita Ekberg again?*
For *Juliet of the Spirits* color was an artistic necessity because the story was born of colors. It was inspired by Giulietta and based on her. I had been thinking off and on of making another film with her; and after *La Dolce Vita* and *8½,* the idea became even stronger inside me. I wanted her to play a character different from Gelsomina and Cabiria, both of whom were inspired by her. Giulietta is the kind of human being and actress who gives birth to and nourishes my ideas. I had also thought of story lines in which she would be a witch, or a nun (half-witch and half-saint), a woman in contact with the supernatural who would live in a weird world, shot against strange and mysterious backgrounds. But I did not succeed in finding the exact image to correspond to a character of this type, until I focused upon the idea of *Juliet of the Spirits.*

But why was color essential?
Because it was an integral part of the narrative texture. It informed the structure, course and characterization of the story; its function was to instill a festive and lavish atmosphere. What I mean is that it wasn't a superfluous superimposition. But I didn't start from any cultural premise, or any pictorial or artistic presupposition, especially because I have always distrusted

any kind of aestheticism. I wanted all the colors of the rainbow without subtlety or sophistication. I didn't rule out the possibility that I might be induced, like Michelangelo Antonioni in *Red Desert*, to paint fields, trees, hills and objects, but above all I wanted the film to turn out like a dazzling harlequinade.

And yet the critics judged your efforts to be a failure in large part.
I won't hesitate to admit that the film's lack of success humiliated and hurt me, to the extent of making me think about the length of a director's creative life. If we leave aside Dreyer, who was a kind of monk and made very few films, or Chaplin, who was more of a circus master, usually the artistic vitality of a filmmaker lasts ten, fifteen, at most twenty years. But I don't believe for a minute that *Juliet of the Spirits* was a semifailure. It's got a lot more vitality than the critics who panned it.

Why did you shoot the film almost entirely in Fregene?
As I've said on other occasions: Fregene is my Genesis. Not only did I shoot *The White Sheik* there and some scenes in *La Dolce Vita*, but also many of my later films were conceived and partly shot at Fregene.

When did you discover the place?
In 1939, a short while after I arrived in Rome. I went with an artist named De Rosa, who worked for *Marc' Aurelio*. It was a Sunday and we left around ten in the morning. But De Rosa was a bad driver and didn't know the way, so we got lost. Around noon we stopped in open countryside, a flat, desolate, endless landscape. The only thing to be seen was a structure by the side of the road surrounded by cypresses and weeping willows. It was a cemetery, a tiny, solitary cemetery with very few graves, but cool, shady and inviting. I was looking in fascination beyond the gate when a gruff voice with the unmistakable cadence of my local dialect boomed in my ear, "What

are you doing here?" It was the cemetery keeper, who came from Santa Giustina, a little village ten kilometers from Rimini. He told us we were twenty-five kilometers from Rome and that Fregene was two kilometers away. A little later we drove up to another gate with a sentry box beside it. Inside was a man licking his thumbs and dispensing tickets. So we had to pay a toll to enter Fregene.

When did you start to spend your vacations at Fregene?
In the second half of the fifties. After I had filmed the end of *La Dolce Vita* there, we bought a plot and had built, to Giulietta's design, a little villa, where we stayed for two or three years, going both in summer and in winter. Fregene is just as enchanting in the winter as it is in the summer. Toward evening the pine forest is invaded by a light mist, which shrouds everything like a lunar halo. In the winter Fregene is the refuge of all the cats along the coast: ravenous packs—mangy, lame and blind—which invade the gardens of villas where anyone is still staying. Each night, on the way back to Fregene from Rome, hundreds of yellow eyes glittered in the darkness, lit up by the headlights of the car. They all had hard, stiff tails and screeched like the cats in an Edgar Allan Poe story. A little scared, I would open the fridge and mash up for them everything that was there. One evening I even put twenty vials of Ferrotin—a tonic I was taking for my health—into the hodgepodge, which made them even more aggressive.

When you left this little villa, where did you move to?
We bought a plot on the south center of Fregene and built a larger house, with two stories, balconies, porticoes, a lawn, rose bushes and a garden. Giulietta grew tomatoes, aubergines, beans; she made jam and tarts. I would go on long walks from the pine forest to the beach and back, which reminded me of

walks in Rimini, with a stormy sea, a leaden sky and that atmosphere of holiday's end that became a recurrent theme in my films. One morning, while I was walking through the pine forest, a fine resounding voice shattered the silence: "Federico!" It was Orson Welles. He asked me for an axe, saying to me, "Why don't we chop down a tree? It's good for the muscles." He lived near me. We promised to meet every morning, to chop down trees, ride horses and swim. But we never saw each other again. I don't know if I would have been able to chop down a tree or ride a horse, but swim—definitely not. I have never swum in the sea, not at Rimini, not at Fregene, nor anywhere else. It's my special form of shyness. As a youth I was very skinny; my friends called me "Gandhi" and I was ashamed to be seen in a swimsuit. I used to remain fully clothed under the sun. And I used to do the same at Fregene.

In which part of Fregene did you set Juliet of the Spirits?
Between the sea and the pine forest. We lived in the Ligurian part of Fregene. In the wilder part of the brushy hinterland I had a little art nouveau villa built in which we shot most of the interior scenes. In more or less the same area, I set some scenes and the finale of *Satyricon;* that is the sequence where the old philosopher Eumolpus, played by Salvo Randone, immolates himself on the shore on a funeral pyre and his friends eat his roasted flesh. But the other films I made between *Juliet of the Spirits* and *Roma—Toby Dammit, Fellini: A Director's Notebook* and *The Clowns*—were not set in Fregene. *Toby Dammit* was a tribute to Edgar Allan Poe, a great favorite of mine ever since I was a teenager. *A Director's Notebook,* which was conceived as an extended interview, was a television feature on the accident-ridden and doomed project *The Voyage of G. Mastorna. The Clowns* was a television documentary on circus performers, who have fascinated me ever since I was a child.

Critics have observed that your Satyricon *has very little to do with the work of Petronius; that it is yet another disturbing tour around your own fantasies. Do you agree?*

Petronius is an old favorite of mine. I read those precious fragments about life in ancient Rome when I was working at *Marc' Aurelio* in the years that spanned the thirties and forties. My colleagues and I wanted to turn it into a review featuring Aldo Fabrizi. We produced a rough draft, but then the project ground to a halt. During the same period I also made a cover design for a new edition of Petronius, but in the end the editor preferred the design of Enrico De Seta. In 1967, when I was laid up in the hospital, through the trials of *The Voyage of G. Mastorna,* I started to think again about Petronius and his *Satyricon.* But the gestation of the film was long and difficult. I had considered at first putting the dialogue of the main characters—Encolpius, Asciltus and Giton—in Latin. I had even consulted Latin experts such as Ettore Paratore and Luca Canali. But in Latin the film would have been hard to understand and I restricted myself to using only certain phrases. That my film might be thought to have little in common with Petronius, I consider more a compliment than an indictment. It is a fragmentary work, full of gaps and obscurities, which could provide me with only some hints toward an imaginative reconstruction. For me, the ancient world is like a nebulous galaxy. Moreover, my interest in history per se is very limited. The film is a kind of essay into the science fiction of the past, a journey into a mysterious world.

Into the mysterious world of your personal fantasies?

My intention was to make a film outside of time, an atemporal film, but it was impossible for me not to see that the world described by Petronius bore a remarkable similarity to the one in which we live, me included. Petronius's characters are prey to the same devouring existential anxieties as people today.

Trimalchio made me think of Onassis: a gloomy, immobile Onassis with the stony glare of a mummy. The other characters reminded me of hippies. It may be that I have also projected my personal fantasies into the film, but why not? Am I not the film's creator? If we gave the film the full title *Fellini Satyricon* it was because another Italian director, Luigi Polidori, had made a version of the work at the same time.

Is it true that you even thought of securing Toto for The Voyage of G. Mastorna?
Yes, I thought of him. I would have liked him to make an appearance, just as he was, without changing him in the slightest. Toto was an actor and comic character, complete in himself. He could play only himself, like Pulcinella.

When and where did you meet him?
When I was a journalist and he was doing warmups and curtain-raisers. I remember he said to me, "You write that I like money and women." Later I met him again on the set of *Where Is Liberty?* and on many subsequent occasions. He also came to my house in Via Margutta, with his partner, Franca Faldini. He was a modern and secular version of God's fool, an amazing marionette, a dazzling gem extracted from the Neapolitan abyss.

How was The Clowns *born?*
NBC, for whom I made *Director's Notebook,* wanted me to work with them again. I proposed a series of projects, including a profile of Mao and a journey with Tibetan monks. But it was difficult for me to get away from Rome, so then I proposed a documentary about clowns. I discussed it with Bernardino Zapponi, my scriptwriter. Later, Italian television got involved. We made a trip to Paris and then, a few days after our return, hammered out the script. It doesn't need saying that I knew

Drawings for The Voyage of G. Mastorna.

Drawings for The Voyage of G. Mastorna.

everything about the circus and clowns. Now it was a matter of translating my knowledge, experience and encounters with clowns into images. But we discarded a lot of the sequences that Zapponi and I had thought up during our research in Paris.

Which ones?

We had thought up a sequence featuring Chaplin, but afterward I didn't have the courage to ask him to do it. I was frightened he'd say no and wished to spare him the displeasure of doing so. But later I put his daughter in the film. We had also visualized a portrayal of the great men of our time in the guise of clowns: Jung, Freud, Picasso, Hitler, Mussolini, Pope Pacelli, Pope Roncalli, Moravia, Pasolini, Visconti.

And yourself?

Yes. I consider myself to be a solemn figure, but also a white clown. Clowns are the first and most ancient antiestablishment figures and it's a pity that they are destined to disappear under the feet of technological progress. It's not just a fascinating human microcosm that is vanishing, but also a view of life and the world.

Roma, Amarcord, Casanova, Orchestra Rehearsal

COSTANZO COSTANTINI: *Did any aspect of the city escape you in* Roma?

FEDERICO FELLINI: A great many things, if not almost everything. In my other films, the themes I handled seemed to me exhausted when I had finished shooting. For example, after making *The Nights of Cabiria* it seemed absurd to me that the Passeggiata Archaeologica was still there. In the same way, Via Veneto was finished as far as I was concerned after the last pieces of scaffolding were dismantled on the set. In fact, every time I walk down it, I'm amazed it's still there; that the Café de Paris, the Excelsior and Doney still exist. The demise of Via Veneto didn't affect me in the least; indeed, I was astonished that it resisted for so long. After shooting *Roma,* on the other hand, I suddenly had the frustrating feeling that I hadn't even touched the surface of the city. It still existed and would continue to exist, fascinating, unknowable, supremely ignorant of the film I thought I had made about it and extraneous to that film. I move about as if I were in a diving suit. I have a curious eye, but it sees only what I want to see, perhaps what frightens me. I had before me an immense subject and I didn't want to drown in it, to end up like a beached jellyfish. I had the Rome that I had imagined as a boy in Rimini, basing my fantasies

79

on schoolbooks, Fascism, Mussolini, Julius Caesar, American films. Then there was the Rome of the *vitelloni*, a kind of Damascus, Baghdad, Nineveh, a pop pastiche of all these confused images and misconceptions. There was the Rome of 1938, the year when I settled in the city: a Rome seen through the thirsty, dazzled eyes of a provincial, with war, Variety, curtain-raisers and the Roman women plump and languorous as odalisques. Finally there was the Rome of the fifties and sixties in all its craziness and explosive tension: a rampant madness, an overwhelming delirium raging amid the city's timeless, inhuman, sirenlike beauty, its palazzi, its shadows, its courtyards, its colors, its absurd and fascinating perspectives.

What had you wanted to include that isn't in the finished film?
So many things. For example, I wanted there to be a sequence on the Verano cemetery, that is, on death as it is regarded in Rome. In Rome even death possesses something of the familiar, the intimate, the domestic. Indeed the Romans call it the "dry godmother," as if it were a relative. They say, "I'm going to visit papà." Later you discover that they went to the cemetery. In Rome the cemetery is like a big apartment building where you can potter about in pajamas and slippers. Sometimes in Rome one breathes an air of profound quiet, as in Africa: there is a different sense of space, another rhythm, another sense of time.

But where are you living? Are you not aware that Rome has become more and more neurotic, chaotic and jammed up?
I tried to depict these aspects of Rome in other films, but I was accused of not liking the city. The neurotic attack, as long as it is not too serious, can be compared to a kind of providence, as Jung teaches. It obliges us to make contact with remote and unknown parts of ourselves. For an artist the pathological aspect of neurosis reveals itself as a kind of hidden

treasure. In another way, Rome is always for me what I make of it, indeed what I remake of my earlier creation, like the reflections in a mirror. On the other hand, Rome is a myth, and myths are perpetuated because they represent the unconscious, like a subterranean journey, a submarine exploration, a descent into hell in search of the monsters that lie at the heart of man. Poets, writers, painters in expressing themselves through their mediums are doing nothing other than recounting their adventures on this journey, the torment of this exploration.

But collective neurosis, the kind one experiences in Rome, produces effects altogether different from those of individual neurosis, of the kind suffered by artists.

Rome is a lot less neurotic than other big cities, just because it possesses something of the African, the prehistoric, the atemporal. It has an ancient wisdom, which somehow saves it from the ills that are killing the great modern metropolises or the postmodern megalopolises. I'm not a Roman, but my mother was, as I've said. She was a Barbiani, a Roman family which goes back seven generations. She helped me to understand the mentality, the psychology, the way of life of the Romans. The first words, the first phrases, the first idioms in the Roman dialect, I heard from her mouth. I could recount an endless string of anecdotes about the calm, the phlegmatic character, the sleepy immobility of Rome and its people.

The laziness of the Romans is a cliché. But if you phone first thing in the morning to speak to a painter, a writer, a sculptor, they're already at work. At seven in the morning Moravia was already writing at his desk. You yourself get up at seven and are already on the move by eight, even when you're not filming.

But clichés do not come about by accident. Just because they possess great wisdom, Romans tend not to waste their energies, or give themselves to laborious exercises. During one of my first days in Rome, I was in Prati and had to get to Via Montecristo, in the Nomentano quarter. I went up to a man who was sitting with his back against the wall, fanning himself with a newspaper, waiting for the gentle westerly breeze that comes in the Roman afternoon. I asked him if he knew where Via Montecristo was. He fanned himself, he looked at me and then he asked where I was from and whether I was from the North. He let out a great sigh. He opened his mouth as if he wanted to tell me the route I should take to Via Montecristo, but then he closed it without saying anything. Eventually he asked me, "But is it really there you want to go?" "Yes," I answered. "It's a long, long way. Who'd want to make such a long journey?" he said to me.

For some time Rome has been compared to Calcutta, Istanbul, Jerusalem. The streets and the doorways of the center overflow with vagrants, beggars, mothers sprawled on the ground with newborn infants, young and old people sleeping in cardboard boxes.
This is another aspect of the city that endears it to me. Rome is being compared not only to Calcutta, Istanbul, Jerusalem, but also to New York, Rio de Janeiro and Mexico City. For someone who practices my profession, it is stimulating to live in a city which is also a "cine-city," in which perspectives, scenery and human miseries recall more ancient civilizations, other epochs, other societies. Before I shot the sequence in the Underground tunnel, which I recreated at Cinecittà, the engineer who was supervising the work took me on a tour of the subsoil of Rome. He was a Dutchman who had built dams, barriers, gigantic walls all over the world. But now he was desperate, to such an extent that many times he was on the point of abandoning the undertaking. The subsoil of Rome was more treacherous than the Amazon jungle: no fewer than eight strata, the deepest at some points more than a hundred

meters from the surface. The seismic shocks from the mechanical mole were threatening to cause the collapse of palazzi, monuments, churches, colonnades, capitals, cornices that had remained in miraculous balance for over two thousand years.

But now Rome is caving in without the help of the mechanical mole.
I'm not one of those aesthetes who maintain that nothing should be done to counter the decay of Rome, indeed that it is better to hasten it. But I do enjoy looking at this panorama of dilapidation, collapse and catastrophe. It gives the city the appearance of a film set, of a stage in the process of being dismantled, of a city that is about to be transported and reconstructed somewhere else. Rome is a mysterious planet that drags everything along in its field of gravity. It is enriched and nourished by its own destruction. This tendency to self-destruction makes all the more apocalyptic the archaeological scenery of the city.

Foreign observers say that Rome has become a "dead city."
Death cannot but be present in a city with one of the most spectacular architectural heritages in the world. It is present not just in the ruins, but also in the severity of the baroque palazzi, in the façades of the churches, in the city's religious rituals. It is present, as I've already said, in the heart of Roman life.

The same foreign commentators say that Rome is culturally dead.
Rome does not need to make culture. It *is* culture. Prehistoric, classical, Etruscan, Renaissance, Baroque, modern. Every corner of the city is a chapter in an imaginary universal history of culture. Culture in Rome is not an academic concept. It's not even a museum culture, even though the city is one enormous

museum. It is a human culture, just because it is free of every form of cultural faddishness, or neurotic trendiness.

Alberto Moravia never tires of saying that Rome is one of the least creative and least spiritual cities in the world. He compares it to Manet's Olympia: *a lazy, inert, impassive courtesan.*

Yes, yes, a big sleepy courtesan, but for the rest I don't agree with Moravia. Almost all the great Italian writers, beginning with him, have lived or do live in Rome. Many Italian painters, sculptors and architects have worked or do work in Rome. Italian cinema is based in Rome. As for the spirituality, Moravia confuses matters a little. It isn't an exterior quality to be sought out somewhere else, but an internal attribute. Either you have it or you don't have it. We search for it outside ourselves only when we are all dried up inside. Rome is also a place of the universal imagination, as Borges says.

How did the Vatican react to the ecclesiastical fashion show that takes place in Roma?

As far as I know, it reacted favorably and with amusement. That fashion parade represented the two souls, or the two contradictory aspects, of the Catholic Church: the pontifical luxury, the dazzling splendor of the gold and silver, the pharaonic pomp of the display; and the most humble poverty, the habit of the mendicant friar, the Franciscan.

Have you ever thought of going to live in another city?

There are so many things in Rome that I don't like: the traffic, the Gogolesque bureaucratic quagmire, the endless expanse of car roofs, the violence. I live in Via Margutta and sooner or later, to get back into my house, I shall have to walk over the hoods of cars or the roofs of the palazzi. But Rome is still endlessly fascinating. For me it is the ideal city, if not quite the heavenly Jerusalem. Where could you recapture the light of Rome? A flash of sunlight through a flotilla of shifting clouds glancing between two cinquecento palazzi is enough for the city to appear renewed in all its charm. And the Roman climate; so sweet, so airy, so cooling? "We're waiting for the westerly breeze," men and women say, standing stock still with an enigmatic air in the streets or the piazzas like a picture by Delvaux, Magritte or Balthus. Rome is a therapeutic city, good for the health of body and spirit. It's a friendly city. It's like the court in Kafka's *Trial:* it welcomes you when you come and forgets you when you go.

As was the case with 8½, the critics have dredged up Proust again for Amarcord. *Have you read him in the interim?*
Unfortunately not.

Some have hailed it as a masterpiece, others say you are just repeating your previous films.
But it isn't a masterpiece, just a minor film, a lesser planet.

You're in humble vein today?
No, no, I'm sincere: some of the praise I have found exaggerated.

In any case, you had promised us the film would be the voyage of a twentieth-century Noah across the ecological flood, but you have given us a totally different film.
Is that a reproach? Oscar Wilde says that consistency is the attribute of the idiot. Life is full of contradictions. At the start I wanted to tell the story of a man who had lost all contact with reality and took refuge in memory, memory as a kind of Noah's Ark. At the same time I wanted to pack up my own little puppet theater. But later it seemed more realistic to me to restore a microuniverse that was becoming undermined by whatever poison it carried within it. And so, rather than

launching myself on my universal flood and putting myself in competition with Michelangelo, Paolo Uccello, or Turner, I dismantled all the original framework and put forward again a little planet rather than a big planet, but still with no hope of salvation.

Are you being precise when you say "put forward again," which suggests a form of repetition?
Of course, it's quite true: I repeat myself and will continue to repeat myself. Indeed, I've always been a director, I've never changed occupation and I don't intend to change. It's like accusing a craftsman or an architect of continuing in his trade. We are often accused of repeating ourselves just when we are changing and growing. Writers and painters who constantly rework the same materials are respected, whereas a director who does is not. I don't see what things *Roma* and *Satyricon,* or *Amarcord* and *Juliet of the Spirits* have in common. I am always myself: however insatiable our curiosity might be, however much we might be able to increase it, a boundary is indispensable. Otherwise we risk going up in smoke, becoming cloud. Each person works alone in his own little garden. If my endowments really are exhausted, then I'll do a film about exhaustion, repeating myself all over again.

But outside there is the shipwreck, the deluge, the apocalypse, while you carry on working in your garden by yourself. Doesn't that seem to you a little absurd?
The apocalypse impends everywhere. You always live in your own time. There's a right way and a wrong way to portray life politically. Each of us does it according to our individual sensibility. If, suddenly inspired, I had tried in a direct manner to represent the catastrophe that threatens us, I wouldn't have been myself, because I would not have used my own idiom. It is easy to have grandiose thoughts: everyone has delusory in-

tuitions. But someone whose vocation it is to tell their story to others, cannot but use their own style, even if it is faulty. It's all a question of style.

But don't you think that by seeking refuge in memory you cease to exist, living like a ghost in your own private Marienbad? Why don't you give up this nostalgia? Why not do something to rid yourself of these memories and so exist and live in this moment, on this day, in this month, in the menacing and chaotic times which press on us? Why not make films about contemporary reality, impending reality?

Mine is not a nostalgic memory, but one of refutation. Before delivering a judgment, one must first try to understand: reality can't be contemplated aesthetically, but reviewed critically. *Amarcord* is an awkward film. How many films have you seen that have given you the same picture of Fascism, the same portrayal of Italian society of that period? I showed the film to President Leone in the Quirinal Palace. I almost felt embarrassed, out of politeness, to show an Italy so poor, so wretched and so ignorant in that residence guarded by the Presidential Guard in dress uniform. The film has a direct relationship with the present day inasmuch as it tends to suggest the danger of any intention—in a less naïve and clumsy but more ominous way—of returning to the same kind of society. Fascism is like a threatening shadow that doesn't stay motionless at our backs, but often lengthens in front of us and precedes us. Fascism always lies waiting in ambush within us. There is always the danger of an education, a Catholic education, which pursues a single purpose: to place the individual in a condition of psychological inferiority, to corrode his integrity, deprive him of any sense of responsibility, nail him to an unending immaturity. Thus, by recounting the life of a village, I describe the life of a country and show the young the society out of which they are born. I show them the fanatical, provincial, infantile, gauche, shoddy, humiliating character of Fascism and that era.

In an age in which young people, adolescents indeed, have thrown over the old ways of thought and behavior in sexual matters and relations between the sexes, you are still insisting that frustrated teenagers should indulge in masturbation.
I don't see much difference between that sinful, distorted, fumbling way of having sex, and the conquests of today. I don't believe any real progress has taken place. Nowadays we are witnessing a frenetic, neurotic scramble for sexual fulfillment, but I don't see any true liberation. We are always victims of Catholic education. I don't know how many centuries it will take for us to be freed from it. I don't know when we shall be cured.

From certain hints it's clear that with Amarcord *you wanted to represent rural Italy as an alternative way of living, as some kind of possible salvation. But contemporary life in the provinces is even more corrupt, squalid and dismal than life in the city.*
I agree. Provincial Italy has become a degenerate form of the city. Things are anticipated or amplified in a frightening way. Certain rituals, like sexual orgies, are assuming a wilder character. Husbands photograph their naked wives and send the pictures to newspapers. It's a further sign of the madness that is taking hold of us all. The countryside is no longer like a nursing mother to us. Of course, in the country the rhythm is different, there is still a sense of time, one feels the presence of the great artists of the past, but the big cities are necessary for the circulation of ideas. As for the provincialism of cinema, each of us can enlarge the boundaries of his own interior space. Turning oneself into a tourist is a pointless exercise. As I've

Amarcord: *The drawing* . . .

always said, I am the worst kind of tourist-witness, because I don't see anything.

In an era like our own, the very attempt to repropose a bucolic, Virgilian kind of poetry can have something tiresome, irritating, if not downright obscene about it. We are presented with a delicate, refined poet reciting under a willow tree by the side of a river or in his ivory tower, while all around him the storm rages and catastrophe approaches.

You don't get any of this in *Amarcord*. What you get in the film is a chilling kind of countryside. You only have to think of the child who tries to kill his brother in the pram. In *Amarcord* you see rejection, dejection. There is an atmosphere of suspense, like a fog blurring the edges of things. But the sense of waste is ineluctable, definitive. Besides, we are already deflated: we no longer control events; they control us because we are exhausted and empty. Opening the newspaper in the morning is like drinking a cup of pure poison, or a glass of sulphuric acid. So why not look at the fog, at a certain kind of light, for an hour a day, away from neurosis and anxiety? That's also life.

Can we be certain that you have finally wound up your personal puppet theater and that you won't make it perform another time?
With *Clowns* I put pay to the circus; with *Roma* I put pay to Rome; with *Amarcord* I put pay to provincial Italy. Now I shall make a film about women and then have done with that subject.

And after that?
I shall sit down watching old age advance and I shall make a film about it.

Why didn't you go to LA to pick up the Oscar for Amarcord *personally?*
Because I was obliged to celebrate the third anniversary of the preparation for *Casanova*. It really did take three years to prepare that film. Dino De Laurentiis had set the project in motion, but then everything ground to a halt over the choice of lead actor, as had happened with *La Dolce Vita.* The producer wanted an American star at all costs, who would ensure the film was enough of a commercial success to at least pay for itself. He put forward the names of Robert Redford, Al Pacino and Marlon Brando. I told him that all three would make the film into the complete opposite of the one I wanted to make, but he didn't pay the slightest attention to my objections. He said, "What do you mean rejecting Redford? He would follow you like a little dog—'Redford, come here. Redford, go there,' and he would scuttle off." "But Redford's isn't the right kind of face," I would object. "Why do you worry about that? Put

him in a mask, whatever one you want," he would reply. "Al Pacino is an extraordinary actor and he too would follow you like a little dog," he would say. "But Al Pacino is one meter twenty high, while Casanova was one meter ninety," I would object. "You're mistaken. Al Pacino has the stature of a giant," he replied. When he didn't get his way, he abandoned the project.

Who replaced him?

Angelo Rizzoli junior. At Cineriz the occasion was celebrated as the return of the prodigal son to his family, who had lent the house luster by bringing to it *La Dolce Vita, 8½* and *Juliet of the Spirits.* But then the project started to take on excessive financial dimensions. The producer recalled that I enjoyed the reputation of being no less a prodigal and sought a budget limit. "What kind of budget can one stick to in a country like Italy, where we aren't assured of our own personal survival for the next half-hour?" I had said to him. And he backed off in alarm. Then Alberto Grimaldi entered the fray. Beforehand he had secured distribution agreements with Titanus for Italy, Universal for the United States and United Artists for the rest of the world. The film entered the production stage. We had salvaged it, all covered in barnacles and mold, from the depth of the abyss. My first thought was to entrust the role of Casanova to Gian Maria Volontè. But subsequent postpone-ments lead to a breaking off of negotiations. So I gave the role of Casanova to Donald Sutherland, a big sperm-full waxwork with the eyes of a masturbator, as far removed as one could imagine from an adventurer and Don Juan-like Casanova, but a serious professional actor. I met him when Paul Mazursky asked me to act in *Alex in Wonderland.* And then, just a few weeks into production, the producer called a halt to the film and dismissed all the members of the cast.

What had happened?

The stoppage was unexpected and incomprehensible. Usually I have certain warnings of what might happen, certain premonitory signs. But this time I didn't have any kind of warning.

Hadn't you consulted Kol, your clairvoyant friend?

No, unfortunately. Alberto Grimaldi had said, "Shooting should have finished before Christmas 1976 and the cost of the film should not have exceeded 4 billion 200 million lire, but by Christmas Fellini had shot only sixty percent of the film and had already spent 5 billion." But that wasn't the truth of the matter. In the first place, no one can tell what a film will cost, not even the producers or the big American film companies. A film is like the creation of the world. Perhaps I won't be believed, but, when *8½* was being made, even a cup of tea that I had offered during the shoot to the wife of the Australian ambassador to Rome was put on the bill. And to the costs themselves you have to add the interest charges, which become more onerous by the day, the cost of publicity, of the launch, and so on. But in the case of *Casanova,* the sums had been inflated.

Who had inflated them?

I don't know, but they had been exaggerated. As for the rest, there's no truth in any of it. The production schedule allowed for twenty-six weeks, from July 21 to January 21. By December 16 we had reached the nineteenth week. Seven remained. But four weeks had been lost for various reasons: two because the sets weren't ready; one because Sutherland had fallen ill; a fourth through strikes. In those few months there had been more strikes than there had been in the Italian engineering sector for the entire postwar period. So really we had eleven weeks left. I had cut the script, eliminating twenty percent of the sequences, so we could have finished the last quarter of the film in six or seven weeks. But all of a sudden this holdup occurred. I really don't know where I found the strength to carry the film to its conclusion.

Isn't it possible that all these incidents happened because, far from liking Casanova, you hated him?
How could I have liked him after I had undertaken the task of reading his *Memoirs?* They are deadly dull, written with such fastidiousness that one never understands what he's talking about. They're just an ocean of paper, more tedious and depressing than a phone book. Even the most beautiful apartments become sterile when described in the style of a court reporter. To give you a visual impression of them, it's as if the Leaning Tower of Pisa had been rebuilt by convicts using toothpicks. But more than through the hatred I bore Casanova, I can't rule out the fact that all these incidents might have happened because I wanted to destroy the myth of Casanova, I who had always maintained that myths were something vital, to be cultivated rather than destroyed. Now the myth was taking its revenge and was destroying me. It's totally incredible what happened: the negatives of the film were stolen, a deed never witnessed in the history of cinema, nor even in the history of crime.

How could you expect to please the public with a Casanova like yours: a bald, glabrous, waxen beanpole, covered with powder and oil, filthy and stinking?
But I had expected that the critics would appreciate the attempt to rid ourselves of a character so disgusting and supine: symbol of the *ancien régime* and the Counter-Reformation; an image of the frustrated, infantile, repressed Italian.

So were you disappointed by the judgments of the critics?
Yes, but I remember them only vaguely.

If you don't remember them I'll give you a résumé. Grazzini, in the Corriere della Sera: *"Casanova remains merely a high display of craftsmanship, even if it has flashes of visionary genius which take the breath away." Biraghi, in the* Messaggero: *"This universe—in an advanced state of disintegration—does not throb with genuine anxieties but sags under its own weight, muddy and stagnant." The radical Emma Bonino: "I literally fell asleep in the cinema."*
I suffer from such severe insomnia that even the remarks of Emma Bonino can't put me to sleep.

Susanna Agnelli: "It is a film against life, full of death."
I congratulate Ms. Agnelli: she has understood the film perfectly.

The feminist Anna Maria Frabotta: "Even Fellini has begun to open his eyes to women as objects."
I would like to begin to close my eyes, not open them.

Germaine Greer, in Tempo Illustrato: *"After ten years of the New Feminism, Fellini dares to present an image of women more alienated and fetishistic than anything one could expect from the most pornographic of porn films."*
I'm sorry for my friend Germaine Greer, but she has not understood that in the film I present Casanova's point of view on women, not my own.

But there are also positive reviews. Ignazio Majore, in Secolo XIX: *"Fellini's view of the eighteenth century is very modern and regrettably topical." Mario Soldati, in* La Stampa: *"In truth* Casanova, *with a message both more simple and more profound*

*than any of the critics have been prepared to acknowledge, is an
innovative film and different from all of Fellini's other films."*
Those are the only two articles that I read.

*And then there's the reaction of the public. "I haven't seen the
film and I shall not go and see it," said a suburban Roman house-
wife. When asked why she wouldn't go and see it, she replied,
"Because all my friends have advised me against it." "This Fellini
has bored me to death," a gentleman from the same area said.
These attitudes are pretty representative.*
The confusion and disconcertedness that the film provoked in
some viewers, what with their disappointment and inability to
express an opinion, are, it seems to me, owing to fairly clear
reasons. The public was expecting that the film would portray
what they already knew and what they had wanted to think
about Casanova. But what did the public really know about
Casanova? Nothing, or almost nothing. No one, or hardly anyone, had read the *Memoirs,* including myself. But there is nothing in the world more resistant to change—and more
unchangeable—than something vague, vacuous, general and
clichéd. It is much easier for a person to change his profoundest
convictions than his commonplace ideas. Besides which, the
public were hoping to be shocked, but only up to a certain
point, with a large share of complicity on my part. Speak ill
of the subject, of course, but not too much: after all it is a
national phallic monument.

*The critics say you have depicted an eighteenth century which is
wholly improbable; that you have turned Casanova into a sordid
lackey of power, ignoring the Enlightenment thinker, the man of
letters, the scientist, in order to transform him into a reactionary
and moribund dummy.*
I hadn't set out to make a historical film; *Casanova* is not
a historical film about the Enlightenment. If my eighteenth

Poster for Casanova *by Giuliano Geleng, 1976.*

century is improbable, I ought to be thanked for it rather than castigated. What was European society on the eve of the French Revolution if not a cemetery? Casanova the Enlightenment figure, the man of letters, the scientist, the great personage—what did he achieve in literature, science or politics? Marxist critics here said that film doesn't help us to solve the problems that are besetting us: but art doesn't resolve problems; rather, it poses them.

How do you answer the feminist critics?
I'm sorry that feminism didn't pick up on the relevance of the film. It takes issue with the very thing that I tried to show in a critical light. How can one not see that sex, *eros* and *agape,* understood and practiced in a certain manner—namely, as narcissism, without tenderness and any real sense of intimacy, any real emotional and imaginative content, without reciprocity; as mere repetition, physical activity, gymnastic display, a fleeting, frustrating, neurotic contact—leads to nothing but death? How can one not see that a man like that can see a woman only as an object? But none of that has been understood.

Then why do you continue to say that the involvement of the
auteur *is not necessary?*
I admire those people—directors, painters, writers, sculptors—
who, when the creative phase has passed, manage to regard
their own work with an objective eye, trying to evaluate what
they have achieved. I have never heard anyone say to me that
their work is worthless. And I, too, can't bring myself to say
it. With *Casanova* I had no pretensions. I simply made a film.
Critical opinion has a minimal effect upon me in my capacity
as a creator. If I had to make *Casanova* again, I would do it
exactly the same. Neither criticism nor self-criticism is of any
use to me; indeed, taking critical opinion into account can be
dangerous for me. After I have finished a film, I feel so emptied
that I risk proving right those who criticize me. But I was
grateful for the appreciation of the film given by Georges
Simenon. In a conversation I had with him in Lausanne, he
confessed to me that he had cried while watching it.

But he also confessed to you that he had had 10,000 women: not
even the most megalomaniac Italian man has told such a tall story.
It's true: he made love every day, several times a day, and paid
for it, of course.

There are rumors that you're about to reconsider the idea of mak-
ing a film in America.
Going to America might prove a godsend to me: such an upheaval, such a transplantation and new beginning might give
me a new lease on life. But not going there is definitely good
for me: by avoiding all that upheaval I at least conserve what
little energy I have left. I could leave with the film already
written and designed, ready to be translated into images in one
of the Fox studios in Los Angeles, rather than in Cinecittà. But
what would be the point of that? Often I think about it as if
it were someone else's problem and I hope that this other

person will go to America instead. Maybe I'll accompany him to Fiumicino and then turn back.

What do you propose to do after Casanova?
In a world in which everything is splitting up and falling apart—children splitting from their parents, husbands from their wives, lovers from their partners, friends from each other, the rank and file from their political parties and unions, people from themselves—I would like to make a film about reunion, about androgyny and hermaphroditism, which represents the ultimate reunion in myth, religion and literature. To me this idea seems to answer a profound need inside all of us, and I hope to realize it shortly. I would like to have a studio like the craftsmen of the Renaissance, to make all sorts of things in it—films, TV programs, trailers, passport photos for friends, portraits, caricatures—producing images nonstop.

Is it true that, besides the big American studios, you have also received offers from Iran and Saudi Arabia?
The Iranians wanted me to make a film about pornography with Bergman and Kurosawa; the Saudis, a film about the Middle East. The Emir of Kuwait said to me, "Think about it, Signor Fellini. If you've achieved miracles with Romagna, just think what you could do with Mesopotamia?" But how can you propose to a director that he make a film about pornography? And yet it was Warner Brothers who suggested it to me. I didn't fully understand what the Emirs wanted from me. Perhaps they wanted me to make a film on the religious and mystical feelings engendered by petroleum. The artists of the quattrocento and cinquecento painted crucifixions for the glory of the Church; I shall hymn the deeds of Cyrus, Xerxes, *The Anabasis,* for the glory of Iran. Now that I am so far from my youth, I think that any kind of excuse is good to fire the imagination and set the creative juices flowing. When you're young

you need faith, anger and a ideological or moral thrust, but when you're getting on, any excuse whatever is good. I wouldn't mind making a news documentary about Kuwait. Its Hilton hotel is the biggest and most luxurious in the whole chain. It has skyscrapers in the desert, oil wells that look like galaxies when seen from the air, like a Ray Bradbury story. I would like to show walled cities eaten by sand and wind, women with faces like leather—new images and sensations. The Emirs tell me that I will have fleets of helicopters at my disposal; they describe them as if they were flying carpets. But I hope that neither they nor the people from Warner Brothers know who Attila is.

There are also wonderful women.
Yes, but unfortunately I shall not be able to take advantage of that fact: as I have already said, for some time now after my tenth fuck of the day I have to give it a rest.

But don't they stone prostitutes to death in that part of the world?
This is the only point on which I don't find myself in agreement with the Emirs. The whore is the true mother of the Italians. We have been raised on the myth of the Mediterranean mother figure, but it has always stayed with us as a myth, never translated into reality. And so, where the reality is lacking, we substitute that dark, mysterious mother, which is the whore. It is the whore who gives us a real point of contact with life. Therefore we raise a hymn, a triumphal arch to her.

Who helps you achieve that tenth orgasm of the day?
I possess an extensive collection of porn-film stills. My friend Groucho Marx presented me with some of them in New York; others we acquired together on Broadway. He showed me an endless stream of them. He asked me, "Are you or are you not an Italian? Then you can't refuse to see porn films." He was

convinced that Italians spent their lives watching porn films and masturbating.

Whereas?
I am almost sixty, but my main problem is still finding ways of assuaging my virility.

You have always maintained that it was reductive to interpret your films in a political way, but now, with Orchestra Rehearsal, *you have given us a political film. What is responsible for this change of direction?*
With *Orchestra Rehearsal* I did not intend to make a political film, but only a film. Every interpretation of *Orchestra Rehearsal* that follows a formula—political, sociological, psychoanalytic, et cetera—is reductive and falsifies the film. This is the reason I don't want to talk about such interpretations and be constrained to choose between one or the other of them.

To begin with, people have asked how it was that at the very moment when the government was under attack, rightly or wrongly, from all sides, you should have invited the representatives of the Palazzo, *from Sandro Pertini to Giulio Andreotti, from Amintore Fanfani to Francesco Cossiga, to be the very first to see the film.*
I have no reason at all to reprove myself for this. It all happened by chance, through a meeting in the street with President Pertini, who told me he had seen *La Dolce Vita* on French television and complimented me on it. It seemed to me only kind and democratic to ask him if he would like to see my new film. I don't consider politicians to be a privileged audience. Many of those who saw the film I had known personally for years. These days politicians are like performers in masks; they are projections of ourselves. We are all in the same boat. And then, how can they go to the cinema unless they are sur-

rounded by bodyguards? The daily life of a politician, under the psychosis of terror, is hard to imagine. An astronaut sent into space is much more master of his life and less isolated than a politician: if for no other reason than that, in the cosmic solitude, he is consoled by the myth of Icarus, the myth of Ulysses.

Here's the point. In the film you show us the members of the orchestra rebelling against the conductor in a confrontation that has all the style of 1968. But aren't you aware that reality has changed and that today they shoot off submachine guns in the streets? The figure of the old musician who takes out his pistol and starts shooting seems prehistoric today.

I didn't want to present a historical essay, nor a political, nor a sociological one. I didn't want to express any condemnation of the union movement. It is a rehearsal, not a history of Italy. A rehearsal whose story is told in a unity of space. The film is also the expression of an unknown aspect of my character and its encounter with the unconscious of the viewer. And it is through this encounter that the impact, the rapport, the strength of emotion occurs.

In La Dolce Vita *you had foreseen, in a kind of premonition, the hard times that would follow that era of delusory and self-confident euphoria. Have you now changed into someone giving advanced warning about the past?*

In *Orchestra Rehearsal* there is the same presentiment I had when I made *La Dolce Vita*. In the film there is a sequence in which everyday, shabby reality—a television interview with some of the members of the orchestra—transforms itself into an infernal saraband. No viewer notices this violent and unforeseeable sequence. Why? Because the viewer is already, in reality, living in this hellish atmosphere. With good reason he could say, "But why is the director showing us what we already know?" It is just this kind of shock of recognition that I wanted to provoke with the film.

In the film the musicians fall prey to a sort of destructive rapture, an anarchic and violent delirium, toward the conductor. But who or what does he represent? Could he not be equally responsible for what happens?
This is a provocative question. If you want to give a social or political interpretation to the film, even as a parable or metaphor, you have to see it as a crisis of an entire society.

Leaving aside the film for a moment, how and why do you think we have reached the present state of affairs?
I'm a director, not a politician, nor a sociologist, nor a psychoanalyst. What I can say everyone can say. There is complete insecurity. What is it owing to? Difficult to give an explanation. We have had an education that looked only to ends, to tomorrow. Tomorrow meant possessions, property. We have never had any direct, immediate contact with life. We don't have a sense of society. The greatest social unity in our country is the family, or the two families, the regular one and the irregular one. We have never been obliged to cultivate our own interior, moral lives. It is always other people who must be honest, responsible, altruistic, never each of us individually and personally. So we live in a society that is the product of terrible injustices, of egoisms so socially stratified that we have become ignorant of them, of crookedness of every kind. Fatal social upheavals await us. But I can't propose any remedy, except to suggest an ultimate, extreme change in our way of thinking. And it must happen inside each of us, at the level of the individual.

How do you explain why no one can give us a clear and convincing account of what is going on in Italy without referring to the "dev-

ils" of Dostoevsky; to the Russian or Chinese secret service, and to the American or Israeli ones; to the theory that terrorism is a new aspect of national and international political warfare? Is it not a basic idea that you cannot combat a phenomenon if you are not aware of it? Is it possible to make progress by blaming 1968 for what is happening today in Italy, as even you demonstrate in Orchestra Rehearsal? *Don't the roots of today's events go back a lot further?*

I'm the last person to give an answer to these questions. But I don't think politicians are in any position to answer them. Perhaps psychoanalysts and sociologists have the answer. Politicians are in a dreadful state these days. They are overwhelmed by a mental stress unknown to analysts and for which a therapy does not exist. It is a new kind of neurotic illness, which threatens their integrity, their private life. They regress to an infantile stage and the bodyguards who protect them are transformed into nannies. How can one hope that men reduced to this condition can cope with the menace posed to us by social conflict, violence and terrorism?

Are we destined then to experience that "shipwreck" that you have already prefigured in La Dolce Vita—*and what's more a shipwreck that shall not in any way be "lavish," "lit by rainbows," but dark and terrible?*

From *La Dolce Vita* until the present I have done nothing but work and practice my craft. Work has helped me to progress, but at the same time it has kept me apart from events, from what was happening around me. I followed events through the newspaper headlines. But even through the headlines I was able to realize that an alienated resignation to the abnormal, the delirious, the monstrous was spreading throughout the country. The most worrying aspect of the situation is the limitless possibility we have to eliminate everything. We have reached rock bottom. We have become empty vessels. Perhaps we have escaped death by a terrifying indigestion, but now we find ourselves in a desperate situation.

Does the possibility not remain for some kind of shock of recognition?
I hope so. It's this sense of appalled recognition that I intended to evoke in *Orchestra Rehearsal*. But I fear that the functional purpose one can put it to, in one sense or another, reduces its emotional impact. Every partisan interpretation damages the film. On the other hand, not even the Moro* outrage, it would appear, has produced a salutary shock to the system. It was greeted with a kind of feeling of redemption: a sin had been expiated. The Catholic myth of sacrifice intervened rather than any kind of collective trauma that might have led to a turning point, a renewal. Myths are protective, but we must confront reality, take responsibility for ourselves, become adults.

Reconciliations and Polemics

Roma had, among other things, one unexpected effect: it reconciled Fellini and Vittorio De Sica, between whom there had been bad blood, as the director himself used to say. Their squabble

---

* On March 16, 1978, Aldo Moro, five times prime minister of Italy and one of the most respected figures in the Christian Democratic Party, was kidnapped by the Red Brigade. On May 9, 1978, he was found dead in Rome after the Italian government had consistently refused to make concessions to his captors. The assassination was condemned by both Western and Communist countries. The parliamentary elections in June 1979 resulted in a coalition government of Christian Democrats, Social Democrats and Liberals under Francesco Cossiga, which remained dependent on Socialist abstention for its parliamentary majority. The parties of the Left—both Socialist and Communist—abstained in the autumn, to allow the passing of draconian reinforcements of measures to deal with the perceived terrorist threat. Such provisions would normally have provoked a public outcry: the fact that they did not indicated the level of anxiety in Italian society.

dated back some ten years. In 1960 *Il Messaggero* had compiled a report on neorealism, interviewing directors, writers and actors. Speaking of Zavattini and De Sica, Fellini had declared:

Zavattini is a poet of the richest resources, capable of gleaning subtle secrets from reality and entirely new perspectives. But I think that he has never really plumbed the depths of the true essence of his personality, because he has never brought his own subject matter to the screen. The collaboration with De Sica, although vibrant with high achievements, is hard to divide into the components of the respective parties; so much so, unfortunately, that I fear Zavattini's most characteristic qualities remain at the theoretical stage, in "poetic" note form.

De Sica, who had contrived great eulogies about Fellini, was extremely irritated. In a letter of July 29 addressed to Emi, his daughter by his first wife, the stage actress Giuditta Rissone, he wrote:

The collaboration between Flaiano, Pinelli and Fellini is easily broken down into its respective components. The clear and sober narrative quality of Flaiano is distinctly apparent in Fellini's films. The dialogue, a little theatrical at times, carries all the trademarks of that talented writer for the stage, Pinelli. And all the provincialism, the mannerism, the symbolism (sea monster, Christ ascending, angel), the charlatanism and the ideological ambiguity are all pure Fellini.

But in 1972, Fellini and De Sica made their peace. After he had seen *Roma,* De Sica wrote a letter to Fellini in which he said that he had enjoyed himself immensely. Fellini replied with a very nice letter, which is now in the possession of Manuel, one of the two sons De Sica had by his second wife, the Spanish actress Maria Mercader.

City of Women

COSTANZO COSTANTINI: *Is it true, as the newspapers say, that* City of Women *was the most difficult, accident-prone, dramatic film of your career?*
FEDERICO FELLINI: The most unfortunate film of my career without a doubt is *The Voyage of G. Mastorna:* I have been intending to make it since 1966 and I still haven't succeeded; I think I never will.

But of the films you did manage to make, what was the most unlucky?
Yes, *City of Women.*

More eventful than Casanova?
Infinitely more. It's well known that I'm not averse to using hyperbole, but I don't exaggerate when I say that what happened during the making of *City of Women* had never occurred since the days of Méliès. Births, deaths, funerals, catastrophes. The "human comedy," or, rather, the "human tragedy." A sequence of calamities, a succession of disasters, an uninterrupted series of unforeseen and unforeseeable events: accidents, illnesses, burnings, short-circuits, explosions, protests, union disputes, strikes, uprisings. A whole compendium of negative

events, or events more negative than positive. Ettore Bevilacqua died, the man who had been my personal masseur and who was a kind of steward to the whole troupe. Nino Rota, my musical director, died. Ettore Manni died, one of the film's two lead actors, the other being Marcello Mastroianni. Dante Ferretti and the cameraman Gianni Fiore had children by their respective wives or lovers. Marcello Mastroianni and the screen-writer Brunello Rondi both lost their mothers. What's more, Marcello had to have no less than four operations on his eye because of an infected sty, which didn't give him a moment's peace. Many electricians suffered burns to their hands or to other parts of their bodies. The executive producer of the film, Renzo Rossellini junior, got married to Lisa Caracciolo, the famous Roman princess, whom he met on the set while she was producing *Notes on the Film "City of Women,"* a feature directed by Ferruccio Castronuovo. I myself broke an arm and had to go around with it in plaster for more than a month.

Pardon me, but is Alberto Grimaldi right then when he says that you are the Attila, or the Super-Attila, of world cinema?
That's a treacherous question. I ought to pretend not to have heard it. However, I'll tell you that *City of Women* developed within a specific atmosphere: a constant tension, an incessant and increasing neurosis of alarm. Every film has its own way of being lived through. We lived through *City of Women* as if we were in the savannah, in a landscape threatened by every kind of danger. But if I think about it now, I have to admit that I got away with a lot, even too much: the attempt to fathom the abyssal depths of the female psyche obliged me to turn myself into a deep-sea diver, and it is a miracle that the sharks only grazed me and didn't also maul and devour me.

So you mean that it is a miracle that you got out of it alive?
Exactly. I ran some mortal risks, ones about which I had had

a presentiment even before I started to shoot. I had a prophetic dream. I saw in a rapid series of frames, all that would happen to me, and which later really did occur. The dream lasted a fraction of a second. I saw an endless expanse of water and myself in the middle of a storm on a little sinking boat, the waves already lapping at my calves, and all around the fins of sharks. A dramatic vision, but one that instilled in me a sense of tragic gaiety, a feeling of religious faith in a portentous event. What can a man think when he sees himself surrounded suddenly by a shoal of sharks? He can think only what I thought: that a helicopter would appear, as in a Bond movie, to pluck me away; or one of those specially trained sharks that unexpectedly turn into dolphins; or a mysterious bird which could grab me away from the jaws of shipwreck and death.

But what happened to you instead in the dream?
At that point I woke up. But when I was about to finish the film I had another dream, which can be seen as an answer to the first one. I found myself in Venice. Beneath me was a canal, to my left a bridge and in front of me Giuseppe Rotunno, the director of photography, the giver of light. Rotunno wanted to reach me, but instead of crossing the bridge he gave a leap, at the risk of falling into the canal. What should happen next? But just when he was about to plunge into the deep, a submarine emerges which takes him on board and brings him to me. We embraced with the joy of two shipwrecked passengers, of two schoolmates who haven't seen each other for ages. The meaning of the dream is clear: as I have said many times, for me cinema is light; it cannot exist without light. Rotunno represented light, the salvation of the film. The film wasn't shipwrecked, we weren't drowned, because a portentous but fundamentally rational event took place: the submarine is a scientific instrument, a product of high technology that can

descend to the depths and come back up again. Rather than a diver, I had changed into a submariner.

Now can you explain the meaning of the film?
As I have said, on other occasions, a filmmaker expresses himself in his films, and once the film is finished, his task is finished. When the film is still just an idea I don't feel like talking about it, because of both a kind of superstition and out of respect for the idea itself. Ideas need to be left in that form of limbo where they appear beautiful and mysterious; if they are removed from that limbo, if they are put into words, they lose their beauty and mystery. When I start to shoot, when I embark on that amazing adventure which is the realization of a film, when I'm inside the process of creation and as long as I am within it, I can talk about it. I couldn't do otherwise than defend it, correct all the errors, lies and banalities that are said about the film. But when the film is finished, when it's about to be screened and enter circulation, I am no longer able to talk about it. The film has acquired its own autonomy, its own independence; it is a creature which can stand on its own and must walk on its own with whatever strength it possesses.

Do you also agree with the theory that a work of art is judged on its own, independent of its author and the circumstances of its production?
I think that to a certain extent the creator must stand aside and abandon the film to itself. If he talks about it, analyzes it, interprets it, he ends up impoverishing it, imprisoning it in a suffocating mesh of concepts. Speaking for myself, when the film is finished I become extraneous, absurd as that may seem; it's as if I hadn't made the film. Everything that one might say would be like a dark screen placed between the film and the audience. Beneath the mass of interpretations delivered by the critics the viewer becomes dazed, confused, terrified—even

before he gets to the cinema to enjoy the images that the film offers. A film is not a philosophical, psychological or sociological tract. It is a series of images intended to provoke in the spectator a more or less profound emotion, at both the conscious and unconscious level. Exegeses, however learned, deprive it of its power. In every case, when I have finished a film, the strongest impulse I feel is to escape as far away as possible. With the passing of the years this impulse has become gradually stronger and now I get annoyed even when I'm recognized in the street; I feel uneasy, I want to run off somewhere else.

Let's get back to City of Women.
I hope the film evokes emotions in you, profound or otherwise.

But man is not merely an emotional organism; he also has a mind that thinks.
What did you think when you saw the film?

I thought that after La Dolce Vita *and* 8½, *the inseparable partnership of Fellini and Mastroianni had reunited to confront* "la femme revolté," *in other words the female universe in revolt.*
And what, according to you, was the result of this struggle?

The Fellini-Mastroianni twins were defeated. It became clear that neither you nor Mastroianni was in any state to understand the world that you confronted, what you call "the deep abyss of the female psyche."
And why couldn't we understand?

Because the two of you had remained more or less how you were in the period of La Dolce Vita *and* 8½, *whereas the female universe had altered radically, bewilderingly.*
You haven't understood anything about the film. You haven't grasped that the dark, unknown, mysterious woman of *La*

III

Dolce Vita, the slave of the harem in *8½,* as well as the aware, self-aware, lucid, rebellious woman of *City of Women,* are all one; always me. I am, simultaneously, both the ocean in tumult and the diver within it.

You can't wriggle out by parodying Flaubert.
But what has that cliché—*"Madame Bovary, c'est moi"*—to do with *City of Women?*

Have you read what has been written about the film? Have you followed the reactions of the public?
I was hardly going to waste my time collecting every newspaper that mentions the film, or hiding in the corner of the cinema to see from their facial expressions the reactions of the public, or hear what they were saying.

Have you read the papers, yes or no?
I've read them and I haven't read them.

Explain.
The way I look at them is rather like a Peeping Tom. When I hold a newspaper and open it at the page that has something about me, I don't hold the page in front of me, but look at it askance, obliquely, from a certain distance, as if what is written there concerned another person with whom one is very friendly but, at the same time, a little distant from. It's not that I do it out of fear or insecurity.

So maybe you do it out of courage, out of a kind of ironclad security. But what do you think about the opinions of the critics and the public's reactions?
The reviews were good, positive, even if some of them seem to me to have been written with a sense of confusion. As soon as you reveal yourself to be completely sincere, you're either

breaking the rules or making yourself incomprehensible. Excessive sincerity verges on indecency. But I'm starting to be something of an elder statesman in cinema; I mean I have certain experience and I don't let myself be caught undefended and unawares by the views of the critics. On the other hand, the critics have always treated me with sympathy, if not with respect. They've never delivered hard judgments on me, not traumatically hard ones. The reactions of the public seem to me even more positive. They enjoyed themselves and left the cinemas satisfied, satiated. The young especially, both men and women, received it well and in the right spirit.

If you keep reading the newspapers through the corner of your eye, you'll run the risk of being taken in by them. It's true that for the most part the critics praised you, even this time, for what they call your visionary power, but they haven't refrained from expressing doubts, reservations and occasional adverse criticism. Even viewers have reacted and do react in various ways, and I don't mean feminists.

Many feminists contributed advice, notes and short essays to the film. We have had a civil, almost elegant relationship. It doesn't seem to me that their reactions were all that unpleasant.

Does what Adele Cambria wrote seem to you civil, elegant? She wrote: "No, Federico, women are not manure for your vices."

She was in fact one of the women who came to me to collaborate on the film. She brought me some little notes, a pretty little essay on feminism, which I partly used. This tiny woman with eyes like fireflies was very nice, and now I can understand her reaction. Perhaps she thinks she's Joan of Arc. Her article has no relevance to *City of Women;* in it she doesn't talk about the film or about me, but about herself, her frustrations and problems. *City of Women* has nothing to do with what she says.

A young woman teacher has said that City of Women *"is the film of a dirty old man and the women in it are the kind that only a dirty old man could invent."*

If that should offend me, it would offend me through the adjective "old," not "dirty." As a good Catholic, to be called dirty seems to me a medal, a distinction, a coat of arms.

Guglielmo Biraghi has said that you are a solipsist.

I must confess that I don't know what the word means, or, at least, I haven't understood in what sense he has used it. Perhaps not even Biraghi knows what it means. But then you are being rather partial: you cite only the negative criticisms. Antonioni, Antonello Trombadori, Lina Wertmüller, Natalia Ginzburg and many others have expressed favorable opinions.

Antonioni has said that in this film you display a disconcerting sincerity, which is true perhaps, since you yourself have said that excessive sincerity verges on indecency. But I can't agree with you on the judgments of the others. Trombadori is notoriously encyclopedic, he gives opinions on everything, but he would have said the same things even if he had been asked to express his opinion on the Marino Wine Festival. Lina Wertmüller should follow the advice of Roman Polanski: never talk about your own films; still less about the films of others. Natalia Ginzburg didn't express an opinion, but delivered a final judgment: "I think it's very lovely. I'm not interested whether it's for or against women. It's very lovely and that's enough!" One could answer her in the same peremptory tone: "I think it's very ugly. I'm not interested whether it's for or against women. It's very ugly and that's enough." They would be equivalent opinions, or judgments.

But I don't want to criticize the critics. It's a pointless exercise and vaguely improper. Making films and making criticisms are two different activities. If at all, I can make only a general observation, a small point: critics don't talk about cinema. The truly cinematic fact is taken for granted. The fact that at a time as shoddy as the present, when American cinema has once again invaded our cinema screens, an Italian director succeeds in producing a film that is, so to speak, handmade, as if produced by an artisan, not by an auteur, but by a master craftsman—that fact is ignored by everyone.

Giovanni Grazzini, talking about the tunnel in the film, wrote: "Better to close one's eyes to reality, better to curl oneself up in dreams, seek shelter there while the train enters the tunnel of old age."

Let's hope that he meant that I was near the end of my career, but not at the absolute end. However, I still have a vague desire to make more films. Reality! But what does this word mean? Each has his own reality. I draw upon my personal reality, upon the dark side of myself, my unconscious.

But your unconscious is inexhaustible!

It's as if you wanted to say, "Are you not ashamed to have an inexhaustible unconscious?" My unconscious is as inexhaustible as anyone else's.

No, your unconscious is different from other people's; it's a bottomless pit.

So many banalities! People even think I said that *City of Women* would be the crowning achievement, the *summa* of my career. I've never said anything so foolish, especially as *summa*, like solipsist, is a word I don't understand and can't even manage to pronounce.

But what, then, is City of Women?

It's a film about women, or about a man who tries to explore himself through women.

So it's a film about yourself? The critics are right?
I haven't done anything other than make films about women,
or about myself, if you want. I was driven by women to make
films. I think with dismay of my friend Francesco Rosi who
always makes films without women. I really don't understand
how he does it. Without women I couldn't do anything.

*But why did you always say until recently that you needed to stay
a grown-up, and yet now maintain that you must always remain
infantile, adolescent?*
Because I have realized that becoming an adult has only one
result: the understanding that becoming an adult serves no
purpose.

*Why previously did you say that cinema was light and now you
affirm that cinema is woman, namely darkness, obscurity, enigma?*
Cinema is light and shade like a woman. How can one describe
darkness without illuminating it?

Why are you so afraid of old age?
I've never posed the problem of old age for myself. This, I
confess, is a form of flirtation. I feel I'm an old man when
people remonstrate: "But no, Federico, you're like a forty-year-
old, a thirty-year-old, an adolescent, a child."

*Don't you fear physical decay with all its consequences? What do
you fear most: aches and pains, toothache, kidney disease, or de-
clining powers?*
Baldness. Every time I wash my hair and feel the blank expanse,
a shiver goes up my spine.

Do you fear creative impotence?
I don't think I've reached that stage yet. It's said I take refuge
from reality, that all I do is dream. Well, now I have agreed

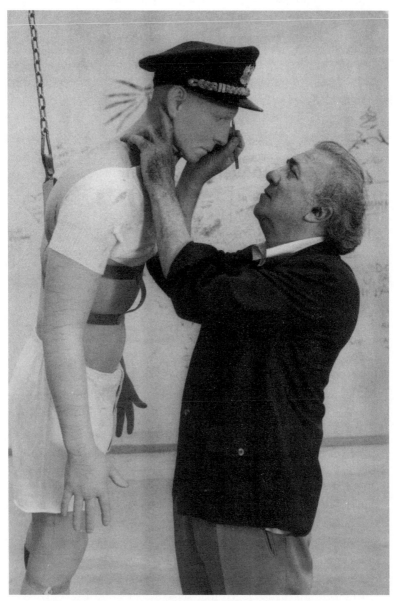

Fellini touches up a mannequin during the shooting of City of Women.
Cinecittà, 1979. (Photo: Tazio Secchiaroli.)

to make a detective series for television. I want to bear witness, as they say, to the dark and tragic times in which we live, to this labyrinthine and indecipherable point in history, and the detective genre seems to me the one best fitted to represent the sense of bewilderment that oppresses us.

You never tire of professing yourself a Catholic. But in what sense are you a Catholic? Do you believe in God, in the immortality of the Soul, in the Afterlife?
These are problems that do not concern me. They are problems for greater personages. I have always lived as if escaping from something, passing from one telephone to the other; I have never had the time to get to the bottom of these questions. Why and in what sense am I a Catholic? I cannot escape from the amniotic sac of Catholicism. How can one manage to say that one is not a Catholic, how can one succeed in freeing oneself from a view of life that has lasted for 2,000 years? It seems to me a little too nonchalant to call oneself an unbeliever as certain friends of mine do. I am not greatly attracted to rebellion, but it is Catholicism that has given me that roguish streak of rebelliousness which redeems me. Catholic ritual acts as a stimulant: it lends a subtle and disturbing pleasure to breaking the rules and infringing the prohibitions that it sets.

This is the traditional psychological mechanism: sin—remorse—absolution—sin, in perpetual cycle.
Call it what you want, but for me it is stimulating.

Are you not afraid of death?
Not at all.

But you do think about it?
As if it were a film. I don't think one can avoid the need to dream about an event that is so unknowable, despite all that

has been written about it by philosophers, theologians, anthropologists. . . . In any case, I can't understand how the younger generation can manage without the mysterious halo that Catholicism projects upon woman.

It doesn't appear as if psychoanalysis has been of much help to you, or that City of Women *was, as they say, a liberating experience for you, leading you to new sets of values.*
They can say what they want, but the pursuit of a woman wiggling her hips, while the great bell of St. Peter's tolls out its admonishing and threatening peals, is an image that still continues to bewitch me.

Of all the adversities that accompanied the making of City of Women, *what for you was the hardest?*
The death of Nino Rota, obviously. Ours wasn't a relationship like all the others, those that are born, develop, grow and decline. It was a friendship that was never subject to any change. The first time we set eyes on each other, we had the sensation of having rediscovered each other. It all happened in a flash. I would often meet him at the Lux, in Via Po; I would notice in passing this gentle, kind, little man always with a smile on his face. He was always trying to leave by doors that didn't exist, although he looked as if he really could have flown out of a window, like a butterfly, such was the magical, unreal aura that surrounded him. He was at the same time totally there and totally not there. In whatever surroundings or on whatever occasion one might meet him, he always gave the impression of having turned up by chance, but at the same time he gave one the assurance that one could count on him.

But where and how did you meet?
In Via Po, as I said. I was just leaving the Lux; he appeared at my side and accompanied me for a long way. Together we

walked the length of Via Po. When we reached the traffic lights, I asked him, by way of a farewell, "Where are you going?" "I was going to the Lux. . . . I must go to the Lux," he replied and turned around. It was just this vagueness in his relations, this behavior, this elusiveness of his that gave him the appearance of a child crossing the Tritone at the height of the rush hour. He was the most precise, punctual and alert man that one could meet. It was as if he was attended by something invisible; he would pass, he would glide over difficulties, over the riskiest incidents as if protected by a magic mantle, an invisible screen. I don't think he ever suffered any kind of setback, although he didn't wear a watch and never knew what day it was, even indeed what month it was. One day he had to catch a plane at eight o'clock in the evening and since he was going to be late, I urged him to go. He went to the airport, but naturally, without being aware of it, he had missed his flight. He asked the girl at the desk, "But when does the plane leave?" "It has already left," she replied. "But it's ten-thirty." "No, it's twenty-thirty." I think that was the only occasion when reality caught him on the wrong foot, when time rebelled against him. For the rest, never a hitch. Perhaps he would arrive at the very last moment, but he would arrive.

What did you two have in common?
Perhaps the vague and uncertain state of mind of those who are always expecting something surprising to happen. The slightly enchanted aura that surrounded him, just like the vague expectation of some marvel, also communicated itself to others. If he was present, you always felt that things couldn't go badly, couldn't threaten or betray you. He was a creature who carried within himself a rare quality, that precious quality which belongs to the sphere of intuition. It was this gift that kept him so innocent, so gracious, so happy. But I wouldn't want to be

misunderstood. He wasn't a kind of little magician. No, quite the opposite. When the situation presented itself, or even when it didn't, he would say the most acute, profound things, with impressive precision, about men and events. Like children, like certain sensitive souls, certain innocent and candid people, he would unexpectedly say the most startling things.

How long did you work together?
Since *The White Sheik.* Between us there existed immediately a complete understanding. Nino had no need to see my films. During the screenings, in fact, he would often fall into a deep sleep, from which he would awake unexpectedly to tell me, perhaps, with his eyes fixed on whatever images were being projected at the time, "What a lovely tree!" Then he would have to replay them ten or twenty times to study the tempi and the rhythms—but it was as if he had not seen them. He had a geometric imagination, a heaven-sent musical gift, thanks to which he didn't need to see the images of my films. When I asked him what were the reasons for the way he scored this or that sequence, I realized clearly that the images didn't concern him: his was an interior world, to which reality had little hope of access. But at the same time, as well as being a great musician, he was also a great orchestrator, capable of organizing a perfect score.

Could you explain more exactly how your collaboration progressed?
I would place myself beside the piano to tell him the action of the film, to explain to him what I had intended to convey by this or that image or sequence and to suggest to him how they should be accompanied musically. But he didn't follow what I said, even if he nodded and said yes with a great display of assent. In reality he was establishing contact with himself, with his interior world, with the musical impulses that he already had within. His most creative hours were those that followed

sunset, from five to seven: those hours favored his t
gift, his inspiration. Unexpectedly, in the middle of a
sation, he would put his hands on the piano and pla}
medium, like a real artist.

It was like being present at a séance?
More or less. It was a real joy to work with him. You felt his
creativity so near at hand that it gave you a feeling of inebriation, the sensation that it was you producing the music. It
entered so completely into the characters, the atmosphere, the
colors of my films as to permeate them with his music. He was
a complete musician. He lived in music with the freedom and
joy of someone who finds his medium spontaneously congenial.
Our rapport was such that we would risk the tightest schedules
and the most draconian deadlines, certain that everything
would be accomplished in time. The assurance that with him
everything would turn out for the best never left us.

Have you any special memories?
One day we were recording in a large hall. Behind a glass screen
were the orchestra players with the conductor; all around were
microphones, console lights, gadgets. All of a sudden, Nino,
on tiptoe, like a ghost, went up to an oboe and added some
notes to the score with a pencil. These were the sort of "miracles" of which he was capable. I find it hard to believe that
he's no longer with us. I cannot distance his presence from me,
the way in which he would keep appointments. He would
arrive at the last moment, when the stress of the shooting, the
editing, the dubbing was at its height. But when he appeared
the stress vanished and everything was transformed into a holiday; the film entered a happy, serene, inspired phase and
seemed to receive a new lease on life. Nino always surprised
me. After having put into the film so much feeling, so much
emotion, so much light, he would turn to me and ask, "But

who is this man?" "He's the lead actor," I would reply. "And what does he do?" he would ask me, adding, "You never tell me anything." I remember thinking, while I attended his funeral, that I could reuse his music not only for *City of Women* but also for the films I would make subsequently, but perhaps it was a thought occasioned by the emotion of the moment.

Yours was a friendship lived in sounds?
For some time now I have preferred the music for certain sequences to be ready before I have begun shooting. This preference of mine was even stronger than usual for *City of Women,* which has sequences that borrow from the genre of the musical. But Nino wasn't well. For some time he had suffered from a bad heart. Despite the tight production schedule, I was reluctant to call him, even though I knew that he would very probably do the job well. For many days he told me he was ready, but still I hesitated. Then I telephoned him: "We'll do the music as soon as I start to shoot." While I was in the studio gallery, I saw him appear before me. He was pale; paler than usual. With a vague tone of reproof, he said to me, "You've turned into a rascal. Surely you don't want to have someone else do the music for *City of Women?*" We made an appointment. As usual, we would see each other at his house in Piazza delle Coppelle. I was just about to leave Cinecittà to go to him when a friend called me to give me the sad news.

What feelings did you experience at that moment?
That he hadn't died, but had disappeared, like a ghost, a sprite, a musical chord. It was the first time I had had a feeling like that: a strange, ineffable sensation of disappearance; the same sensation he had given me when alive. After more than twenty years of collaboration, what I remember as his most distinctive quality was this lightness, a kind of miraculous presence-

absence. Needless to add that, in my opinion, he was one of the greatest contemporary composers of film music.

Is it true that you are going to direct Aida *at the Teatro Comunale in Bologna; that you have decided to shoot a film in America; that you will make a detective series for television?*
Opera has always held a great fascination for me. It is a kind of Italian ritual, an emblem of Italianness, our most accurate reflection. It has gone on throughout Italian history: the Wars of Independence, the struggle for Unification, Fascism, the Resistance. It is the form of spectacle that most resembles us, that most directly expresses our psychology, our mentality, our sense of style. It's as inaccurate, superficial, shoddy, distracting, stupefying—that is to say, as Italian—as one can imagine. Furious passions, ferocious vendettas, unimaginably exaggerated affections, unbelievable plots, swashbuckling exploits, insane libretti, costumes hired from funeral outfitters, nonsensical lighting, conductors at odds with the orchestra, singers who start running just when the music reaches its best point.

So you could have given us a better portrait of Italy than you did with Orchestra Rehearsal?
One evening I saw a production of *La Traviata* on TV. A frenzied event. The cameramen went back and forth on the stage looking like men awaiting the birth of a child, zooming their lenses in on everything: on the carpets on the floor, on the performers' shoes, on the nails in the flooring, on the singers' gold fillings. A shot of a box of laundry powder wouldn't have looked out of place. They never stayed still. The foreground scenery overflowed the screen: one could just make out that the tenor was from Caserta, the soprano from Venice. Anyway, notwithstanding the massacre of the production, because of the faces of the singers and the fact that I was alone, I sat there transfixed for the whole evening.

Would it be quicker for you to complete the direction than to explain the reasons why you probably won't do it?
I tried to do it, but in reality the opera is already made, or unmade, like Italy. It will go well enough as it is, with all its errors or horrors. It's already the finished article. What could I add to its circuslike quality, its stature as Verdi's super-spectacular, that *Aida* does not already possess? Ever since I've been making films I have received requests from every corner of the world to produce an opera, but I have never found persuasive reasons, not even the emotion that comes over me at the thought of the great festival to be held in Bologna next Christmas. To invite me to direct an opera is like asking me to direct a solemn mass, a pastoral songfest, a procession, a military parade or a funeral procession. The other day the director of Covent Garden came to me, for the fifth time, and tried to persuade me to direct something. He said to me, "Covent Garden is not like La Scala or the Metropolitan, the Paris Opera or the Vienna Opera; it is a free and uninhibited theater, famous for having staged completely unorthodox versions of classical opera. You could do whatever you want." But I wasn't interested.

If you won't direct Aida *at Bologna, will you direct a film in America instead?*
In this case, too, it would be quicker to make it than to give the reasons why I am reluctant to make it. During my stay in New York, where I had gone with Marcello Mastroianni to present *City of Women,* I went to see a musical one evening. It was called *42nd Street.* I thought it would be a revival of all the musical reviews of the period, but instead it was a very tedious show. And so after a while I left and wandered about, defying the crush of people, the fear, the threat that pursued me. A bewildering anthropological panorama. A livid, greenish, neurotic, psychotic, schizophrenic atmosphere, in which people

moved as if they had landed in mysterious spaceships, the most bizarre beings in the universe. Women who approached like hot-air balloons, little faggots sheathed in black satin pants wriggling like lizards, groups of children frightened out of their wits amid a terrifying bombardment of sounds of every kind. Anyway, in the midst of this gigantic, chaotic, fearful torrent of people, sounds, cries and laments, a little man with a velvet cap like Raphael and a seraphic expression, as if in a state of grace, was painting Broadway by night.

Wouldn't the result be an extraordinary film?
But how? Reproducing Broadway as I saw it that evening? What purpose would that serve? I could reconstruct it only in the studio—that is, I could try to reconstruct the emotion it had provoked in me, but to do that I would need my own theater. What would be the point of setting one up in New York when I already have one ready in Cinecittà, Studio 5? But for the moment everything is on hold. I don't know what to do. CBS has suggested that I film *The Divine Comedy*. The script already exists; Ezra Pound himself had worked on it, using the translation of Longfellow. But it wouldn't be a film, but, rather, a space mission, a galactic operation. The economic scale of the film would be enormous, because of which my participation—the participation of a director who intends to leave his mark on what he does—might appear improper.

So will you do that detective series for television that you talked about some time ago?
I don't want to do any more work for television. Television is destroying everything.

The Sixty-Year-Old Syndrome

The appearance of *City of Women* coincided with what psychologists, or psychiatrists, call "the syndrome of the sixty-year-old": the sixty-year-old realizes with a kind of "obscure dread" that the future is dimming before his eyes, inducing in him a subtle and perverse depression.

Perhaps in order to combat this syndrome, in the autumn of 1980 Fellini celebrated the publication by Einaudi of his book *To Make a Film:* a miscellany of memories, notes, asides, events, meetings through which he reviewed the course of his career as a film director.

"I had never expected I would become a director," he confessed, "but, from the very first day, from the first time I shouted 'Camera! Action! Cut!' I seemed to have always done it, and knew that that was what I was and that was my life."

In the book, Fellini confirmed his status as an original and engaging writer, gifted with a vast power of observation. Going back to April 1967, when, stressed-out by the battles with producers over *The Voyage of G. Mastorna,* he had fallen ill with pleurisy and was recovering in the Salvador Mundi clinic, he wrote:

Especially when I'm taken into the radiology room, I feel like an object, a thing. The room, with its cold lights, seems like Mauthausen, or even like a mixing studio. Faces float past along the corridors, silently. Sometimes, the nuns give injections without waking you up, like the henchmen of Cesare Borgia. Then you see them from behind as they disappear into the gloom. . . . At five in the morning, it is still dark. Sister Burgunda comes with black veils like a bat, a rubber tube between her teeth and a great basket of specimen tubes. Like a vampire she says, "Can I have a little of your blood, Signor Fellini?" . . . In those days I was convinced I would die of a heart attack, because I was afraid the production of *The Voyage of G. Mastorna* would be too much for me. "Liberate man from the fear of death." Like the sorcerer's apprentice who defies the sphinx, the ocean depths, and dies there. "It's my film—I thought—that is killing me."

In the paperback edition of *To Make a Film* there is a preface by Italo Calvino entitled "Autobiography of a Spectator." In the essay, Calvino maintains, against the prevailing opinion, that Fellini was a fundamentally realistic and true-to-life director. He writes:

> What has been so often defined as the baroque style of Fellini resides in his constant forcing of the photographic image in the direction that leads from the caricaturist to the visionary. But always keeping in mind a very precise representation as the point of departure, which must find its own more eloquent and expressive form. This is particularly evident in Fellini's images of Fascism, which, however grotesque the caricature, always retain the flavor of truth.

Also in 1980, Fellini received an unexpected tribute. The American director Joseph Losey wrote to him: "Dear Federico, just to tell you that last week on French television I saw again *La Dolce Vita.* What a wonderful film! Cheer up!" Fellini replied: "Dear Joseph, I never watch my films again and when a friend tells me he has seen one recently, I always give a start, as if I had discovered all of a sudden that I hadn't paid my taxes, or that the husband of a beautiful woman has found out everything and is looking for me."

The Cinema Is Finished.
And the Ship Sails On

COSTANZO COSTANTINI: *For some time now you have been saying that cinema is on the brink of collapse, that it is about to end. On what do you base your catastrophic diagnosis?*

FEDERICO FELLINI: In the course of the summer I conducted a direct personal experiment. In company with the producer Renzo Rossellini, I made a tour of eighteen Roman cinemas, first-run and repertory, central and suburban, during the prime-time period, namely, from half past six to half past eight in the evening. I went from one cinema to the next with a kind of increasing inebriation, exaltation. Ruin, catastrophe and apocalypse have always given me a sense of excitement. I was so excited and exhilarated that I would have visited every single other Roman cinema. Renzo was also excited but in a different sense, owing to the impression of real disaster. We pulled apart the curtains, looked at the screen and cast our eyes upon the auditorium: hundreds and hundreds of empty seats, like blind eyes, deserted as the holds of a beached ship. Only in four or five cinemas did the audience exceed the number of staff. It was a sight that has its own kind of fascination, as if wrapped in a science-fiction glow. It gave us the impression that the earth was suddenly depopulated while machines continued to function by means of their own inertia.

By what criteria did you choose which cinemas to visit?
We chose every type of film house and cinema in every quarter
of the city, in order to have a representative sample. From the
center we gradually moved out into the suburbs, but the situation didn't change. We seemed to be witnessing an exodus,
a mass migration, an enormous diaspora. The equipment was
intact, the ushers all in order, the seats, the lights, the projectors
working, but the public was no longer there, it had moved to
another planet. We made out some dark shadows, certain isolated shapes. We felt like going up to them to see if they were
real human beings, rather than funeral dummies put there by
the manager so as not to frighten off any potential patrons.
The cinema managers were surprised at our surprise. The public no longer existed.

But it was summer. People were at the beaches or at the campsites.
No, because the restaurants were packed, the streets were
jammed with cars, cars full of people, men, women and children. I don't know where people go, maybe on safari; now
even postal clerks go on safari with their wives and children,
but not to the cinema. To go to the cinema today is like going
to the Colosseum to see gladiators and Christians torn to pieces
by the lions. It's not just a matter of impressions. The figures
are alarming: in the opening season the audiences have fallen
by forty to forty-five percent.

If it is true, what are the causes?
I don't know, I wouldn't know what to say. But how can one
not consider that device which, by pressing a button, shows
you forty films one after another? Television, violence, the fear
of thinking, of facing reality. How can one make a family leave
their house? Father is in his underwear, the wife is in her slip,
the children are sprawled on the sofa or on the floor, all in
front of the television, which provides them with films of every

kind, the whole of cinema from its birth to the present day. What's more, there's that exaltation that pressing a button gives them, the feeling that they are controlling the world. Bergman has always intimidated them? Oh, well, they press a button and cancel him, annul him. Antonioni has always made them uneasy? Well, they press a button and get rid of him. It is a deliverance from any kind of frustration, the celebration of the most brutal collective vendetta. It's as if they were saying, "But, Fellini, who do you think you are? You're nobody. In fact I destroy you. I press a button and you are no longer there." Not to mention the violence that rages in the suburbs. Hooligans who laugh sarcastically during the film, who taunt couples and piss in the aisles. In one suburban cinema some spectators set fire to the auditorium because they didn't like the film.

But aren't there reasons other than television. Does the kind of cinema that has been made in Italy for the last ten years really have nothing to do with it? Does what is called the image culture have nothing to do with it, and the bombardment it subjects us to obsessively?

Of course they are relevant. The Italian cinema of the last decade has sunk to a shameful level. On one side porn in all its varieties, on the other an absurd and idiotic ideological agenda that has nothing to do with cinema. Cinema is something else. The banalities that have been pronounced upon cinema in Italy in the last decade are not encountered in any other country in the world: monumental imbecilities, interminable interviews in the papers, terribly embarrassing voltefaces. The very same people who took issue with the Golden Lions now hurry to collect them; they go to Venice to readvocate cinema even in its junk form, just the kind of cinema they detested a few years ago. But the most insidious thing is the bombardment to which we have been subjected for over

Federico Fellini draws on a wall a character from And the Ship Sails On, *1983.*

twenty years. The so-called image culture is disastrous. The eye is assaulted, corrupted, tormented. This carnival has shown us everything, the whole history of the figurative arts, every possible series of images. This infernal vortex has made the eye pop; it's no longer able to grasp and appreciate the images that the filmmaker presents it. The cinematographic image is deprived of its most profound meaning, its magical, dreamlike, mysterious quality. It is deprived of its secret charm, which takes its nourishment from the obscure relationship that each of us has with the unconscious.

Does the ticket price not have some effect?
The increase in cinema ticket prices is, proportionately, a lot less than the increase for many other consumer items. In general, the ticket cost has little influence.

In America, television started by destroying the cinema and ended up being its salvation. Do you think that the same thing might happen with us? You yourself have made Orchestra Rehearsal *with RAI TV.*
No, I don't have great faith in Italian television. In America, television has saved cinema because it made itself the mediator between big business and cinema: through advertising, it takes money from the multinationals and hands it over to film production. But in Italy this isn't possible. If by joining the forces of RAI, French television and German television, one succeeds in putting together a billion and a half, it's a miracle. And then again, if you make a film with RAI TV you go crazy. The mechanisms are so complicated, the executive changes so convulsively, that before you've finished the film you've had to speak to ten, twenty different people. The machinations of the different political parties are incredible.

Anyway, it's not true that the public has disappeared. American films are cashing in. In only three days The Empire Strikes Back *took in about 100 million lire in Milan.*

Of course, some films can survive, but the success of *The Empire Strikes Back* is not owing to the film. It is a phenomenon of visual delirium, just as electric guitars cause an acoustic delirium. It is a stupefaction that hinders the ability to think, which reduces individuals to purely sensory, animal organisms, like those who walk the streets wearing a Walkman, hammered senseless by lethal rhythms. We no longer have time to think. It is a collective delirium. I haven't seen *The Empire Strikes Back,* but I have seen *Star Wars.* I saw it in Chianciano. But I don't know what it was, I really do not know.

In short, we're heading for disaster?
I repeat that the image of cataclysm has always fascinated me. After the shipwreck one can make a new beginning. The fact that all the old certainties are crumbling makes me feel young. There's something intoxicating about the end of one thing and the birth of another. But I think it's going too far to talk so much about cinema, to place so much emphasis upon it. Cinema isn't everything; it's just one of many cultural elements. The crisis, the earthquake threatens everything. And anyway, why are there so many cinemas in Rome? Why 104? Are there that many films to see? In my opinion, it would be much more in the interest of cinema if there were only ten film houses— not even open at the same time, or throughout the week. Ten cinemas in which real films could be screened, made by authentic filmmakers. Or it would be better still if only four or five remained open, screening films of the past, maybe with their ancient director, mummified in a wheelchair, displayed as a simulacrum to the visitors in the cinema museum.

If your diagnosis is correct, does it not follow that it is all the harder to make a film today?
Making a film at present is like boarding a plane without knowing where or when it will land. Since the journey lacks a purpose, a route and a destination, the only thing to describe is the journey itself.

Is this what you plan to do with And the Ship Sails On, *the film you are preparing at Cinecittà?*
Two months ago, when President Pertini came to visit Cinecittà, both Franco Zeffirelli and Sergio Leone welcomed him in sumptuous, magnificent reception rooms; whereas I had to be content with greeting him in the street like some unemployed person pretending to beguile the time by watering flower beds. Do you want to know why I changed studios? It wasn't because Zeffirelli was making *La Traviata* in No. 5. I had changed a lot earlier, in October or November 1979. I moved from Studio No. 5 to Studio No. 4. It was my choice, a completely free decision of mine. I wanted to do something new and startling, to mark a new turn in my career. But I achieved only one result: while I used to make films, well or badly, in Studio No. 5, in Studio No. 4 I didn't create anything. In fact, the whole team was laid off *en masse.*

You produced nothing because of the usual financial difficulties?
No, not for that reason. I had so many producers that I no longer knew who I was speaking to, especially because many of them came from the Orient and spoke inscrutable tongues. It was like the Tower of Babel. I made nothing because I didn't like the last producer, simple as that. He was an Armenian named Golan. He ate spaghetti piece by piece, as if they were streamers. Wasn't that a good enough reason to have nothing more to do with him? But there were others. One day he said to me, "Signor Fellini, I have pondered long upon the pro-

found nature of cinema, the medium of film, and I have come to the conclusion that a director is not necessary." I can't say if he said this to get me to reduce my fee or because he really meant it; whichever, I had my lawyer give him an appointment to sign the contract, but made damn sure I didn't attend. Why go if the director is not necessary?

But why did you then move from Studio No. 4 to Studio No. 1?
As soon as the film had come to nothing and the whole crew had been laid off, what was the point in staying there? I don't think that if I had stayed it would have marked a turning point in my career.

So now you really will make the film and it really will mark a turning point in your career?
I hope so, if the shipowners stop persecuting me. They come to me from all points east and west. I am invited to every port in the world, from Hong Kong to San Francisco. They are all hoping that I choose one of their ships. The other week I went to see a ship at Genoa. The shipowner said to me, "Take this one, Signor Fellini. It has everything, even a chapel, a baptistery and a priest. If one of your actresses gives birth during shooting, you can baptize the child right here." He treated me as if I were the Navy Minister. I became seasick, even though the sea was calm. I asked him, "How long will it take to get the ship to sea?" He replied, "Twelve to fourteen months." That was longer than I intended to take in shooting the film.

In which sea will you shoot the film?
In the sea off Sardinia or Sicily, but I don't know how I'll do it. I suffer from seasickness; even when the sea is still I'm afflicted with anxiety, nausea, dizziness. For *Satyricon* I directed the sea scenes from a helicopter, as if it was a Bond film.

What have you been doing all this time, since 1979?
I've sat at street corners, seeing how the world changes, how cinema has changed. At street corners you see everything: the tramp, the thief, the prophet, the assassin, the mystic, the predictor of apocalypse, the bankrupt, the suicide. It is the only way to grasp how the world is changing, in what direction things are going. Thus, from my vantage point at street corners, I realized that cinema was changing, that it was no longer what it was, it no longer had anything in common with the cinema I used to produce in the past. Meanwhile all around me I heard the clanging of the invaders' gongs, of Attila, of Genghis Khan, of *Star Wars,* of the electronic directors, of the Apocalypse. It's all owing to television, which goes for the maximum effect while asking for the least response. In order to satisfy an audience of the Television Age, cinema must make the greatest possible hullabaloo. When the explosion is over, it no longer exists—like a firework.

But aren't you due to make another film for television?
Working with television is completely impossible. You achieve more standing at street corners than going into the offices of television executives.

But have you actually overcome the problem of finance?
I'm expected to perform a miracle: for one of my films the capital must appear, immediately achieve payback and then magically show a profit. It's an alchemical experiment that even the world's greatest magicians can't pull off. Besides, I have so many producers that to list them all in the credits would take an hour.

So the film will last a week.
More or less. The film has already been translated into every language. In English, *And the Ship Sails On;* in French, *Vogue*

le navire or, in argot, *Vogue la galère.* I don't have the German title off pat, and experts in comparative semiology are working on the Chinese translation.

What is the story of the film?
We've known each other for so many years and you still ask me such silly questions? Why do you want to force me to tell tall tales? I can tell you that at the moment I'm deliberating who will play the lead. I have two or three answers, international and home-grown, so to speak. For an international solution, I can't decide between Michel Serrault and Jack Lemmon. On the home front, there's Paolo Villaggio, Ugo Tognazzi or Graziano Giusti, a theater actor who has the right face. Of the Italians, Paolo Villaggio would appear to me the most interesting. Tonino Guerra and I wrote the script three years ago. We knocked it out in the twinkling of an eye during the August holiday in order to secure the advance, certain that the second installment would never come. The film will cost $6 million. I can also tell you that I feel in great form. Making a film protects me from every ill. When I put on my director's uniform, so to speak, I'm out of danger. Once, I arrived on the set with a galloping fever, but as soon as I looked through the lens it went away. When you're filming, you feel like yourself again, a director, without age, outside of time, without infirmities, invulnerable.

Does even your hair grow back?
That's the only miracle that my directorial persona can't perform.

And what of Studio No. 5?
Bordellos open where churches once stood.

And the Ship Sails On *has now been launched. The film is in the cinemas, but the public is disconcerted. Can you explain the meaning of this?*
I wish that in the foyer of every cinema there was a poster saying: "There is nothing except what you see." Or: "Don't look for a hidden meaning; otherwise you won't see what's in front of you." *And the Ship Sails On* is a film that suggests or authorizes every kind of question: Is 1983 like 1914? Are we on the eve of a new catastrophe? Where does it come from, the battleship that fires on the *Gloria N.?* What is the significance of the rhinoceros? At the start of the film the director pays homage to Chaplin, but then withdraws into the studio: has he therefore come out of himself to deal with social reality, or has he turned back to plunge into the depths of his own ego? et cetera, et cetera. To reply to all these questions I would have to be witty, but I can't be witty all the time—it's actually rather difficult and I can't manage it. The film simply tells the story of a voyage by ship to scatter into the sea the ashes of a famous singer from the twenties. Some friends have told me that it is a terrifying film, that it possesses an obscure menace, whereas I think it has a basic cheerfulness all its own.

That's as may be, but your state of mind is very close to the one that characterizes Orchestra Rehearsal.
I don't think that state of mind has ever left me. What's new about what has happened since 1978? Has anything occurred to give us new perspectives, ones less alarming or catastrophic? The film is the product of a series of coincidences, some recognizable, others obscure. Living in a country like Italy even the most detached filmmaker cannot fail to absorb the tragic sense of insecurity that weighs down on all of us; cannot fail to be touched by the fears, the rumors, the dismal feelings that are in the air. And all this, willy-nilly, cannot but be reflected in what he does in his films.

Has your sense of impending catastrophe abated in the meantime, or are you still as pessimistic?
Questions that aim to turn me into a kind of auteur always make me feel very uneasy. In *And the Ship Sails On* I expressed more or less sincerely, more or less artificially—I say artificially inasmuch as a film, as a work of art, is always artifice—the sense of dismay that possesses us. Fear of worse to come is a state of mind or a presentiment we have entertained for a long time and it doesn't appear to be about to leave us. You only have to open a newspaper to realize this. The other day the newspapers reported on their front page that an atomic bomb detonated over Moscow would cause between 50 and 100 million deaths. What a totally irresponsible way to give out news. Between 50 and 100 million, almost indifferently, as if it wasn't a matter of human beings living on this earth, but objects or inhabitants of an unknown and improbable planet. All this is terrifying. We are living in the most delirious unreality, a monstrous world where everything is deprived of its reality.

Monstrous like the rhinoceros that sails on the Gloria N.*—which makes one think of the monster in* La Dolce Vita, *or the enormous steel ball that demolishes the buildings in* Orchestra Rehearsal?
I don't think there's any similarity between the rhinoceros and the monster that appears on the beach at the end of *La Dolce Vita*. A symbol is a symbol inasmuch as one cannot explain it, inasmuch as it goes beyond concept and reason, and contains irrational or mythic elements. Why would you want me to explain it? In any case, if the rhinoceros has any meaning, it is one completely opposite to the monster's. The monster in *La Dolce Vita* was a mirror of the degeneration of the hero, whereas the rhinoceros in *And the Ship Sails On* could suggest the following kind of interpretation: the only way to avoid disaster, to not stumble headlong into catastrophe, could be that which leads toward recapturing the unconscious, profound

and healthy part of ourselves. It is in this sense that one might explain the phrase "drink of the milk of the rhinoceros." But it's still a case of rather crass explanations, just as crass as the parallel between the rhinoceros and the monster. Something of the imagination, if it is authentic, contains everything and has no need of explanation. I couldn't say by what paths the rhinoceros came into my mind. It is one of the most fascinating animals in creation and a testimony to the earliest forms of life. Thinking of the rhinoceros I thought of an unusual, concealed, mysterious and ancestral creature.

Salvador Dali says that the horn of the rhinoceros, that is, the unicorn of antiquity, is a symbol of chastity. Perhaps you're converting to chastity?
Not yet, even though I am now sixty-four. As a form of defense, to exorcise the fear of being sixty, when I was fifty-five I said to myself, "I shall now think of myself as sixty or sixty-one." Age is a mental problem. It depends on how you feel about it. I don't feel that much different.

Your films certainly don't help us to renew our faith in ourselves. In And the Ship Sails On *the Austro-Hungarian First Minister repeats the story that one can't trust the Italians.*
It's a line he has to say because he fears for the life of the archduke. He's angry with the captain of the ship because he has taken the Serbian refugees on board. As a matter of fact, it is a Serbian terrorist who throws the bomb onto the ship.

An ending that is certainly not happy.
Despite the ending, I think the film is happy, so much so that it made me want to make another one, to embark upon another voyage, even if it wasn't to be *The Voyage of G. Mastorna.*

A New Triumph

After the disappointment caused by the critical reception of *City of Women*, Fellini recovered with *And the Ship Sails On*. Presented out of competition on September 10, 1983, at the fifteenth Venice Film Festival, the film was a real triumph for its creator. Along the route from the Excelsior Hotel to the Palazzo del Cinema, Fellini was cheered as never before, with frenzied enthusiasm. Veterans of the festival recalled that only in the "golden years" of the Lido, when Luchino Visconti screened his most famous films there, did such things happen.

For more than two hours Fellini was made the target of a relentless, frantic, implacable assault by fans, reporters, cameramen and the public who had streamed into the Excelsior foyer for the occasion, as well as those outside and along the street. "How can I inveigh against them if I myself created them?" he said as soon as he arrived in the hotel at about half past eight in the evening. But perhaps not even he imagined in the fifties that one day they would behave again in such unrestrained fashion toward their creator. The director was protected by a double escort—several young minders drafted in from the production company, Gaumont, and the police who controlled public order—but that only caused the triumphal march to stop more often and for the crowd to erupt in uproar.

The screening of *And the Ship Sails On* was followed by spontaneous applause, which ended in a standing ovation.

The reviews of the critics were like hosannas. Giovanni Grazzini in *Corriere della Sela:* "Every film of Fellini's is a surprise, but this time the surprise is great. It's more a matter of the style than of the theme. That Fellini has been ill-humored for many years, unhappy with himself and the world, one knew. But one could never have guessed that he could remain so young in spirit as to renew his language in such a substantial manner as to render it almost unrecognizable." Franco Peconi in *Bianco e Nero: "And the Ship Sails On* represents a turning point. Sadness and melancholy are no longer the motives for creation: images and film itself are. If behind the viewfinder there was an eye longing for truth, that truth enters wholly into the expression and assumes fully its own artistic life. This is a Fellini who achieves a greater classicism, with respect to his own style of filmmaking."

The film and art historian Pier Marco De Santi also drew the comparison between Fellini the designer—specifically Fellini the designer of his own films—and Eisenstein. He recalls that in *How I Learned to Design,* the Soviet director confessed to never having followed any school of design and to having taught himself, imitating the sketches and drawings of the great European humorists who spanned the eighteenth and nineteenth centuries. Eisenstein said, moreover, that he considered the making of rough drafts in "humorous vein" an essential stage between the initial amorphous idea of any mise-en-scène and its definitive theatrical or cinematic realization. He saw to it that the design of a character or of a scene was put down on paper as a kind of summary of the "dance steps" he had to follow as a director, with ever more complex visual rhythms, proceeding in parallel with the different interdependent phases of production, from the set to the cutting room. It is the same procedure that Fellini followed, even though the Italian director had never read *How I Learned to Design,* nor taken as models the great European humorists of the eighteenth and nineteenth centuries.

Fellini, of course, had been drawing since childhood; he was a born draftsman and drew all the time, both before and during production and even when the film was finished. It was only natural that he should design his own films: the characters, the models, the scenes, the costumes, the surroundings, the shots. Design was for him the first, immediate, concrete visual translation of his ideas and came before any overall conception of the film, before the script and the production.

Ginger and Fred, Intervista, The Voice of the Moon

COSTANZO COSTANTINI: *Is it true that the few prints already prepared of* Ginger and Fred *are kept under guard in a darkened room, protected by security guards in bulletproof armor, as if they were copies of the Holy Shroud?*

FEDERICO FELLINI: The pirates are lying in ambush. The pirate video copies of *City of Women* and *And the Ship Sails On* were already in circulation before the film was released. I wouldn't even let my dearest friend see *Ginger and Fred;* it's the only way I can feel safe in this period of interregnum between the completion of a film and its release. At this point only the film technicians should be working on the film, but that isn't the case. Everyone continues to apply to me, when I should be having nothing to do with it. They pester me without respite. Sooner or later I will even end up selling the tickets at the box office.

In jest it's said that you are still giving priority treatment to the great and the powerful, at the highest level, as you have already done with Orchestra Rehearsal.

When I had the Lifetime Golden Lion awarded to me in Venice, I promised President Cossiga a screening of *Ginger and Fred* at the Quirinal Palace. Quirinal protocol decided who was invited. I had suggested only the names of two writer friends, Pietro Citati and Giorgio Manganelli, but only the former came. Nobody had seen the film before, except for the RAI TV executives and the projectionists, who usually talk in loud voices during the screening about Roma or Juventus, drowning out the sound.

It is a fact that the first review of Ginger and Fred *was not written by a film critic, but by that man of the palazzo, Prime Minister Andreotti, who in the past had denigrated Italian cinema.*

The editor of the *Corriere della Sera,* Piero Ostellino, had called Andreotti the same evening, at the end of the screening, to ask him to jot down his impressions of the film. I was understandably embarrassed. But Andreotti was very able: he wrote about the film without indulging in cinematographic critiques.

How come the film was shown in France, Germany and America before it was shown in Italy?

The reason is very simple, or very complicated. It is not a discourtesy toward my country. *Ginger and Fred* is the fruit of a collective production on an international, if not planetary scale. It was financed by Alberto Grimaldi, who for some years has been resident in America, by the French, the Germans, the Turks and by organizations of every kind, public and private, national and multinational. All I can say is that I'm glad to have made it. It is a film about our contemporary life, as long as that phrase doesn't sound presumptuous. A film about television, or, rather, the inside of television. A film that contains an unusual love story, at least for the kind of cinema I produce. I enjoyed making it and I hope that others, too, will enjoy it. I have taught it every trick of seduction and I hope it knows how to use them.

It's rather difficult to seduce the youth of today, as you yourself have said on other occasions. There are plenty of other films that seduce them.

I wasn't referring to young people, or not only to young people. Cinema proprietors talk only about the youth market. They ask, "But has Fellini thought of the youth market?" What is the youth market? Those who through their calling are driven to tell stories, to express themselves, know by instinct that to do so means to communicate. But they don't think of social categories, they don't imagine the cinema divided according to professional status: at the front the high-school students, then the stamp collectors, the housewives, the fans of Sampdoria, at the back the postal telephone employees and the fashion models, et cetera, et cetera. I always regard with great amazement those who profess to know what the public wants, what the youth market wants.

Why after twenty years have you felt the need, the longing, to have Giulietta once more in one of your films?

Ginger and Fred was a story written for her. It was part of a series of six stories about women that were meant to have been directed by me, Antonioni, Zeffirelli, Dino Risi, Francesco Rosi and Luigi Magni, but then difficulties arose and the project came to nothing. And so I thought about expanding the story I was to have directed and turning it into a full-length film. It possessed a wealth of situations that lent themselves to amplification. As a film it had a more convincing rhythm.

You attack television and yet you use it in this film.

It's hardly the case that television is particularly generous toward those like me who try to highlight its power of plagiarism and the disastrous effect it has on its viewers.

Poster for Ginger and Fred *by Giuliano Geleng, 1985.*

But it financed Ginger and Fred, *a film that is a direct and ferocious attack on television, in particular television advertising and those deadly commercial breaks that, in your opinion, break up and destroy a film.*

The agreement with television for the financing of *Ginger and Fred* was not my work, but that of its producer, Alberto Grimaldi. I had no contact whatsoever with the television executives. In the same way, Franco Cristaldi and Gaumont signed the agreement with television for *And the Ship Sails On*.

Intervista *portrays Cinecittà as a fort besieged by Indians, armed with television masts rather than spears. But at the same time you yourself make television commercials. All the newspapers have mentioned the ones you made for Campari and Barilla.*

The financial contribution from television covers only the ti-

Poster for Ginger and Fred *by Giuliano Geleng, 1985.*

niest part of the cost of my films and, on the other hand, the films are subsequently exploited by television. As for the Campari and Barilla ads, I don't disown them, anything but. I enjoyed making them. It's an experience I recommend to everyone. To tell a story in a minute or half a minute, while concealing the product and transmitting in a subliminal way advertising messages, isn't such an easy matter. It's an experience I would repeat, especially since they pay handsomely. But unfortunately they don't ask me any more. Perhaps they are apprehensive of some censorious attitude on my part, or perhaps it's because I had direct contact with Campari and Barilla and the agencies took it amiss. In any case, I am adamant when I insist that commercials destroy a film, that advertising is a new type of cataclysm, like the lava that destroyed Pompei, perhaps more dangerous than the atomic bomb itself. It destroys a human being's intellectual integrity, just like the new cinema that comes from across the Atlantic.

There's something disloyal about your behavior toward television; television pays you, or finances your films, and you slaughter it, a bit like Goya did to Philip IV and his family.
It's not like that. Television finances my films, or co-finances them, in an attempt to salvage its soul. It would like to give proof of its intelligence, its liberty, its tolerance.

But you are not tolerant on your part.
Yes, of course. The hotel in which part of the action of *Ginger and Fred* takes place overflows with television, ever ready to ambush the characters. The whole film is constellated with televisions spewing out commercials, talk shows, gossip about gossip, to the point of bewilderment and stupefaction. At the climactic moment of the film, when Ginger and Fred are on the point of making their entrance to do their number, there is an explosion of commercials. For me, the most fascinating aspect of television is the implacability with which it can scrutinize a human face, and implicate millions and millions of viewers in this disturbing and brutal process. Television fastens on, spies on, transfixes a face in a way that is shameless, cynical, sadistic, fierce. It's something that no other medium can achieve: neither cinema, nor theater, nor photography. Only a great writer could perhaps achieve it, but only indirectly, through the mediation of literature. Television falls upon a face like an implacable probe, like an X ray, a laser. If I watch television, it is because of this terrifying power it has.

In reality television has granted you a kind of "license to kill," which in Ginger and Fred *and* Intervista *you use freely and to the full, with rage, disdain and fury. Are you satisfied with* Ginger

Posters for Ginger and Fred *by Giuliano Geleng, 1985.*

and Fred? *How do you place this film in the sphere of your filmography? Of all the films you have now made, which do you prefer?* It's difficult for me to say, especially because I hardly ever watch my films again. Every film corresponds to a precise moment, both objectively and subjectively. Personally, disregarding the approval they have obtained, trying to be passionate and detached at the same time, I would put *8½ first, then La Dolce Vita, Amarcord* and *Ginger and Fred. Ginger and Fred* represents me as I am today.

Has no new dazzling idea yet emerged from that limbo which you fall into after you have finished one film and are waiting to begin another?

I still haven't been fired up by an idea. I would be happy to do anything whatever. I would like any kind of project, even a totally foreign one, to be proposed to me. The desire to create is vital in itself. Work for work's sake. It is not so much the result that counts, as starting the endeavor. As I have said before, making a film is like making a journey, but what interests me about a journey is the departure, not the arrival. My dream is to make a journey without knowing where I am going, maybe never arriving anywhere, but unfortunately I can't manage to convince the banks and the producers to accept this idea. When I have nothing to do, between one film and the next, I like to meet—partly through curiosity and partly just in case—all the people who declare that they are willing to realize my next project. We usually meet the most extravagant characters at the Grand Hotel or the Excelsior. Without fail they wear white linen suits, even at Christmas, even in the snow or during a hurricane. They propose that I set my next film in the Azores or in the Samoan archipelago, telling me that such locations are eminently Felliniesque and that I couldn't find anywhere better.

You persist in saying that the cinema is in crisis and that television is destroying it, but meanwhile your films continue to enjoy success. Intervista was acclaimed at all the major festivals, from Cannes to Moscow, Locarno to Montreal.

At Cannes, surrounded by thunderous applause, so as not to disappoint the crowd, I almost attempted levitation, ascension.

Joking apart, it was an emotional evening. I realized that the film had a power unknown even to me.

And in Moscow did you achieve ascension? Did you rise like a figure of Chagall's into the vault of the Kremlin?
In Moscow I attended only the prize-giving ceremony. The atmosphere was identical to the one twenty-five years ago when I went there for *8½*. I even recalled it in a short speech. Then there was Khrushchev and "the thaw"; now there is Gorbachev and *glasnost*. Then Khrushchev was dealing with Kennedy; now Gorbachev is dealing with Reagan. But the problems are just the same: the two great world powers trying to overcome the differences and the mistrust that separate them, and a director who always makes the same film. Then, a director who didn't know what film to make and got worried about it; now, a director who doesn't know what film to make and doesn't give a damn. A remarkable coincidence.

What were your impressions of the Kremlin?
It's something unimaginable. We progressed through the magnificent rooms of the tsars like a marriage for three: the Minister of Culture to the right, I to the left and Giulietta in the middle. The dazzling white of the plasterwork, the glare of the precious stones; then, at the end, a huge window which gave onto Red Square under the setting sun, and a sky between turquoise and pink. A mysterious, invisible orchestra was, like an organ, resounding the music of my films. A vision, a mirage, a hallucination. Incomparable magnificence. Nothing like the Oscars and Hollywood.

Have you also attempted levitation on account of the reception the Italian critics and public have given to Intervista?
What pleases me most is the sympathy with which it was received. Almost a feeling of solidarity. I feared that it might be

seen through a telescope, but, instead, it was viewed at close quarters, with warmth, as a special, anomalous, colloquial film, a kind of public confession, between friends, if not a kind of collective psychoanalytic session. It is a film created as by parthenogenesis, made by itself, as the fruit of a life dedicated to cinema. I believe the public participated in this coming together while waiting for the storm to pass over and work to start again. Naturally, since it is a film about the cinema, it was received differently at festivals than it had been in ordinary venues. There is the same difference between a Mass celebrated in St. Peter's and a Mass celebrated in the ordinary churches in the city.

You don't think you were rather cruel to Ekberg?
I shall never cease being grateful to her and above all admiring her. She has spirit, wisdom and humility. The grace and goodwill with which she agreed to appear in *Intervista*, in contrast to her glorious image in *La Dolce Vita*, moved me. For that purpose, Marcello and I had visited her in her villa in Castelli Romani, where she lives like a rural goddess, serene, tranquil and imperturbable, without the passing of the years troubling her in the least. Then we remembered the experience of *La Dolce Vita*. It may be that I was a little cruel to her, but it wasn't part of my intention.

Some have said that you, a great director, are not quite so great an actor.
I've never pretended to be one; I've never put myself forward as an Italian Laurence Olivier. I've always been an actor rather by accident, whether in Rossellini's *Miracle*, Mazursky's *Alex in Wonderland*, or in *Intervista*.

Why did you not include in the film the "vision" that greeted you when you went to Cinecittà to interview Osvaldo Valenti, one of the actors in Crown of Iron, *directed by Alessandro Blasetti?*
I've recounted that incident so many times; it seemed to me a little predictable.

But it was the very first time you had been to Cinecittà, which would become your second homeland, if not your only one; and it was a lovely story.
Crown of Iron was shot in what would become my studio, Studio No. 5. Alessandro Blasetti had had it built in order to shoot the film there. At the time, I was a journalist and the editor of the paper for which I worked sent me to interview Osvaldo Valenti, an actor much in vogue in those days, something of a star. Valenti was standing on a large two-horse chariot whose wheels bristled with deadly sabers. Above all the chaos—enormous horses, armored cavalry, towers, bastions and propellers that stirred up huge clouds of dust—I could hear a powerful, harsh and thundering voice. All of a sudden, in ominous silence, the immense arm of a crane began to rise into the sky, higher and higher into the dazzling glare of the sun. Someone lent me a telescope and up above, at a dizzying height, seated in a chair firmly secured to the crane platform, immaculately dressed—shiny leather leggings, an Indian silk scarf around his neck and a helmet on his head—and equipped with three megaphones, four microphones and a score of whistles, I beheld Alessandro Blasetti.

Is it true that it was that sight which gave birth to your idea of becoming a director?
It was on that day that I first realized what a director was, but I didn't think at the time that one day I might also be a director.

Blasetti has said many times that the picture you painted of him is a bit too picturesque. It is true that he had leggings, something on his head, a handkerchief around his neck, a loudspeaker and a whistle, but the image of some kind of Jove thundering among the clouds is a product of your imagination.
Blasetti seemed to me like an ancient ruler, a biblical personage, the King of Kings of the cinema.

Blasetti says that you are the King of Kings of the cinema.
He has always had great affection for me. When *The White Sheik* was trashed at the Venice Film Festival, he was one of the few filmmakers to come to my defense.

Did you know that Marcello Mastroianni was also in Crown of Iron? *He was an extra.*
No, I didn't know that. It just goes to show that we were destined to meet each other.

Awaiting your revolutionizing of television, you are revolutionizing Italy: in The Voice of the Moon *you have built a new city.*
A town, not a city.

You have constructed a discotheque like no other in the world.
It was very difficult constructing a discotheque that would seem totally new after everything that we have seen on film and television. We have seen every kind of disco: galactic, science fiction, lunar. I wanted to build one without smoke and strobe lights, without an air of catastrophe and apocalypse. But in the effort to stage a wholly new one I ended up going back to smoke and strobe lights, to that atmosphere of stellar collapse and cosmic cataclysm. Strobe lighting is like the batting of eyelids: it transforms everyone into robots, into a mechanical or automatized crowd, prey to a collective psychomotor disorder. No contemporary town could accommodate a disco like

this. To build that town, I turned myself into a master builder, a craftsman, an architect and town planner. I built a town of the most heterogeneous style, at once as unusual and obvious as possible. A medley of styles: medieval fortresses; Renaissance palaces; art nouveau cafés; Fascist, modern and post-modern buildings. But seen as a whole it ends up becoming invisible, like the objects we see before our eyes every day; or the incessant flow of images that television pours over us each day, but which cancel each other out in a kind of automatic annulment.

Does this town reflect contemporary Italy?
Yes and no. After I had built it, I had to people it and I did so with people at once imaginary and real, the kind we see all around us today, and then set about observing them. But it can't symbolize fully contemporary Italy, because it possesses no regional character. It is a transnational town, so to speak. It has much of the chaos and delirium one comes across now in all parts of the world. All together, it suggests such a series of well-known motifs as to lose any specific connotation, any personal character or identity. It is so banal and transparent that it borders on every possible dimension. Everything in it is recognizable and nothing is, inasmuch as there is no longer an individual relationship with reality, with the emotions, thoughts and dreams that reality ought to arouse but no longer does.

The strains of The Blue Danube: *do they symbolize nostalgia for a vanished world?*
The Strauss waltz is summoned up nostalgically by the former prefect, who in the film embodies order, authority, hierarchy, ceremony, officialdom, and for whom the discotheque and the music that rages within it are the kingdom of evil, perdition and the collective madness of today. The former inmate, on the other hand, finds himself at ease in this new kingdom. He

is a Shakespearean sprite, like Puck in *A Midsummer Night's Dream*. He is a creature out of the Brothers Grimm, a pierrot. But he is also Pinocchio; also Leopardi—or Leopocchio, as Benigni calls him.

Are these the two contrasting aspects of your own personality?
Every character, every situation, every element in the film is, to a varying extent, an expression of the personality of the director. Even the discotheque. If Villaggio represents the moment of the "return to order" in the face of raging chaos, Benigni represents the seminal importance of creativity, imagination and fantasy; of that transitory, ambiguous, indecipherable but yet wonderful and thrilling experience that is life.

Did you really make up the film day by day?
Not only did we not have a script, there wasn't even a treatment. For all my other films we had a treatment at the very least. But for this one, nothing. Only don't think I invented and improvised everything. The improvisation that is supposed to characterize my work is a myth. A discotheque like that one can't be built on the spur of the moment and neither can a new town. Making a film is a massive undertaking, like putting a spaceship into orbit.

On the various occasions I have visited you on the set, I have noticed that you take great care about the costumes of the actors. What is the importance to you of costume? What significance does fashion in general hold for you?
The dress is a component of the character. Everything that the characters in my films wear—suits, dresses, ties, waistcoats, hair, vests, gloves, overcoats, raincoats, et cetera—serves to characterize them, to give them an identity and to define them psychologically. Nothing is accidental. Everything is chosen with this purpose, down to the last detail. Colors are very im-

portant. Just think of the colors of the waistcoats that Gogol's characters wear, or that Gogol himself used to wear.

But when dressing the characters in your films, do you get your inspiration from fashion in vogue at that time and from the designers of the period, or from those of the past?
A filmmaker invents his own fashion style. If one invents the characters, one cannot do anything other than invent the clothes they wear too. Yes, of course, one uses costume designers. Costume designers of extraordinary talent have always worked with me: Piero Gherardi, Danilo Donati, Piero Tosi, Maurizio Millenotti and Antonello Geleng. I guide them with sketches and explain the psychological makeup of the characters, and they design the costumes.

But do you follow fashion; do you know designers and go to fashion shows?
I follow the fashion world absentmindedly, as is my way with everything. Of course, I have always known fashion designers, starting with Schubert. I've known Coco Chanel, Balenciaga and Yves Saint Laurent, some of whose shows I've attended and whose workroom I've visited. Obviously I know Valentino, Armani and Versace. How could one not know them? They are the new superstars of the "society of spectacle," the objects of what is now termed the star worship of the masses. But I have never been inspired by them when choosing the clothes for the characters in my films. There are no direct references to their work in my films. It is all invented by us, by me and my costume designers.

The cardinal's fashion show in Roma *is all your own invention?*
Absolutely. Danilo Donati and I thought it up, in collaboration with the painter Rinaldo Geleng and one of his sons, a painter like his father. Danilo Donati is a set and costume designer of

genius. He possesses a rare quality: with the poorest materials he can produce the most gorgeous costumes, as in *Roma, Satyricon* and *Amarcord*. Rinaldo Geleng and his studio, namely, his two sons Giuliano and Antonello, did the pictures that hang in the hall where the cardinal's fashion show takes place. Along with Donati, Piero Tosi and Antonello Geleng also worked with me on *Amarcord*.

But it would be difficult for something of contemporary fashion not to enter somehow into the costumes the characters in your films wear.

It could be that something does enter, especially through my costume designers, but there is never a specific reference. When I am struggling with the expressive requirements of my films, I turn into a researcher, an archaeologist, a historian of style, but always at the service of the figurative necessities of the film. These necessities oblige me to be informed about current fashions. For every film, I gather up all the bits of information that my absentminded and reclusive way of life normally prevent me from knowing, but then I put them to very sparing use.

In your last film, The Voice of the Moon, *the boys and girls who throng the disco wear the same outfits as the groups of Punks and Metal freaks who live on the outskirts of Rome and invade the city center every day: fake tiger jackets, dog collars, spiked hair, studs, rings and earrings.*

Many of those young people just turned up on the set as they dressed normally, at our request. But the others were tricked out in that fashion by Maurizio Millenotti. It was he who disguised those angry adolescent suburban girls as Nefertiti, Cleopatra, Bathsheba, Queen of Sheba, just as it was he who disguised their boyfriends as Teuton knights, as new crusaders of madness and death.

But did these disguises reflect everyday reality, the fashions that prevail today?

No, no. That stylistic code, from the medieval to the space age, was invented by Millenotti. The fashion that is all the rage in the suburbs of the modern and postmodern megalopolis is already so excessive and extreme that it is difficult to depict it as it is in reality.

Benigni and Villaggio were dressed by you or Millenotti? That day I visited you on the set, I noticed that you were straightening out with your own hands the raincoat Villaggio was wearing, just before he made his entrance into the discotheque to dance The Blue Danube *waltz with his mad old wife.*

I'm not as meticulous as Luchino Visconti was, but I pay great attention to detail. In the film Villaggio stands for order, even if in a manic sort of way, but at that moment his raincoat was a little crumpled, which would look particularly odd for a man of such iron principles.

And what designer clothes do you wear? Do you also sometimes wear flashy waistcoats, like Gogol?

I'm flattered by the suggestion of a comparison to a writer as original and gifted as the author of *Dead Souls*, but I dress any old way. Saul Bellow says that today only bank clerks try to look like artists. I don't use stylists. In Rome there are shops where they make suits of various sizes, ready to wear, with trousers turned up. These days I hardly ever do so, but in the past I used to go into one of those shops, put on a suit and, if it fitted well enough, I would take it, putting in a bag what I had been wearing when I went in.

But on the set you dress up as a director, with cloaks, waistcoats, scarves and the enormous hat you use as a substitute for your legendary outcrop of hair.

If ever I dressed up as Fellini, it was without the help of stylists and costume designers, even if they were people of great talent.

What did you take from Il Poema dei Lunatici, *the novel by Cavazzoni that inspired a great deal of* The Voice of the Moon?
Perhaps my response would be more helpful if you were to invert the question and ask me what Cavazzoni's novel drew out of me. What I mean to say is, as is natural, one's reading, memories, encounters, rages, nostalgias, good intentions and resentments can all stimulate and provoke the reflowering of some idea that was always there. This is what happened with Cavazzoni's work. In addition to the way its unsettling originality and intricate narrative attracted me, it recalled to my memory the countryside of my grandmother, Fraschina, and the beasts in the stable, the days and nights, the trees, the stones, the clouds, the storms, the seasons, the entire magical and fearful world of that great silence that descends on the fields at noon. I was also reminded of the Greek myths, the film on Pinocchio, *Till Eulenspiegel* and *Le Libere Donne di Magliano* by Tobino. Now I don't know if all these ideas and characters are present in *The Voice of the Moon,* but some distant echo, some fleeting shadow of those ancient projects has here and there, more or less unconsciously, fed the film. That's not counting the ancient, fertile and inexhaustible source, *Mastorna,* which still emits signs of life from the abyss into which it was cast.

With this film, you were resolved above all else to make people laugh. Do you think you succeeded?
To make people laugh has been my greatest aspiration ever since I was a child. In the third year of primary school we had a teacher called Giovannini, a big, fat man with a mustache who had operatic pretensions. While I was doing an impression of him, he grabbed me by the scruff of the neck and, holding

me in midair like a cat, roared, "What shall we do with this clown?" I wet myself in the excitement of having merited such a glorious epithet. I don't think I have ever again in my life met someone who sent me into such raptures and ecstasies as that stocky, gracious little toiler in the circus, the clown Pierino. Not even in Paris, when I met Chaplin at the theater.

Did the great Chaplin not have much effect on you?
I saw only the mop of white hair, the dazzle of a toothy and aggressive smile, and then his tiny hand covered in liver spots like sequins. "My God, you are so young," I think he said to me in a hoarse, metallic voice. It almost seemed like a rebuke. But he couldn't say that now; I think I'm older now than he was then, during our only encounter.

Of all your films, which one do you consider the most entertaining?
I can't really say. I have tried to remember and represent the clown Pierino in all my films. For example, Richard Basehart, in the character of the Fool in *La Strada,* was something of a tribute to that little "Augusto" in the peasant circus who, like all true circus artistes, was a tightrope walker and bareback rider.

Did Villaggio and Benigni prove themselves to be the two "comic geniuses" you called them before you started shooting?
After having tried for so long, I rediscovered Pierino, someone exactly like him: light, very funny, moonstruck, mysterious; a good dancer, a mime artist, who made people laugh and cry. He has the fascination of characters in fairy tales or the great literary works. He makes any landscape believable; he is a friend of ogres and princesses and talking frogs. He's like Pinocchio. Now I'll tell you who he is: Roberto Benigni.

The ninetieth anniversary of the birth of cinema falls this year: are you not excited by this event?
It is a meaningless anniversary. I could understand the celebration of its centenary, which might invest cinema with a little of the solemnity of events that have something to do with eternity. But this sudden celebration of its ninety years has the shady character of the announcement of a disgrace that, if it has not yet arrived, is almost at the gates. It's as if they lacked the courage to tell themselves that cinema is already dead and are preparing themselves in some way for this shame with the rigmarole of these celebrations. It seems like an obituary notice.

But it doesn't look like cinema is about to die or is in its death throes, even if it is going through an unhappy period.
Yes, but what's the purpose of asking oneself if it is still alive? It seems to me that it's always talked of now in funereal terms and so, frankly, I don't wish to participate in this event.

Perhaps it is as you say, but when the time of the celebration arrives, you won't be able to refrain from taking part.
If you really insist, I am obliged to say that I don't understand clearly what is really happening in the cinema and that it appears to me to have changed greatly in all structural aspects, in both its organization and distribution. What was the cinema for me in the past? The cinema was a dark room with a wall at the back in which there was a little square aperture from which a luminous beam came out and widened onto a large white screen. On it appeared actors in garish makeup who moved their lips without saying anything, enigmatic, mute. It was another world, another life, everything that we didn't know about and that perhaps we could see only in dreams. And along with these vast images and enormous faces, which we seemed to watch from the distance of a few millimeters, a mysterious rustling emerged from that bright rectangle like a ceaseless

whispering of words we didn't understand. That rustling said everything, took the place of the words the characters should have uttered, showed us our dreams, and aroused the dark and shadowy side in each of us. The new technical resources have removed from cinema all its powers of hypnotic, silent fascination.

Unfortunately one cannot turn back, even if, on this occasion, you were fully justified in returning to your origins, to the silent screen and the first films you saw in Rimini as a boy. How did cinema change subsequently? How was it when you grew up and started out on your career as a director?
I am not a theorist or a historian of film. For my generation cinema was a mythic phenomenon that assumed the dimensions of the great events of existence. Beyond its cultural and visual aspects, it was part of life, like engagement, sex and marriage, snow and Christmas.

Other generations have followed yours and in the meantime cinema has changed radically, as you yourself say. How has the cinema's present predicament come about?
I can't talk of cinema in abstract terms. For me speaking about cinema is like speaking about myself, about my life, which by now is completely identified with cinema. What I did before I started to make films was nothing except preparation for what I would do later, namely, directing. I don't have sufficient detachment to analyze all that has happened and is happening in the cinema. However, I harbor a certain skepticism about its state of health, either through the havoc wreaked upon it every day and every hour by television in general and the private channels in particular, or through this laborious pursuit of innovations that are completely artificial with respect to the correct and natural way to see a film—like the introduction of the various forms of stereo sound, which are designed above

all to disturb the aural texture of the film by making voices and sounds swirl around your head, behind the seats, under the floor, from the box office, from outside the auditorium, from everywhere, except from the screen where the sole and magical focal point of the narration lies. All these systems merely pander to the jaded ears of a dull public, incapable of perceiving silence or whispers. And, in short, because the public seems to me to have been corrupted by a host of undiffertheyentiated stimuli from so many mass media, it becomes ever more incapable of participating in the ritual of the projection, the ceremony of the darkened auditorium with that concentration, suspense and expectation without which neither art nor an audience exists.

So you are confirming the apocalyptic predictions you have made in the past?
I no longer wish to prophesy about the cinema. We haven't heard the last of its centenary celebrations, which, if only because of the solemnity of the word, will restore to it a little of the dignity that it seems to have lost at the moment. Paradoxically, Italian cinema was healthier during the period of the great adventurers, people like Peppino Amato, Dino De Laurentiis, Carlo Ponti and Angelo Rizzoli, who were successful at producing films in the grand style, which stood comparison with Hollywood productions. Today the film industry in Italy no longer exists.

The reality is that cinema has changed since the epoch of the great adventurers cited by you. Whether or not it is owing to television, cinema has become something different. It is an electronic, "high definition" product of big business. But you seem reluctant to accept this change, to experiment with the new technologies and make use of the new processes.
No, I haven't experimented with the new techniques. Obvi-

ously, I am aware of the experiments attempted by Michelangelo Antonioni in *The Oberwald Mystery* and those of Peter Del Monte in *Giulia and Giulia*. One of my cameramen talked to me at length about the latter. These techniques, which come from Japan, import a greater stereoscopic effect to television images, but transferring from magnetic tape to 35 mm cine film is a very laborious process. The result is never certain. One risks losing the best of all one's shots. I don't see the benefit to be had from it.

Are you not tempted to try?
No, to be honest. I am still faithful to the singular charm of the cinematic spectacle, as a dream, a vision, a creation of the imagination. I have faith in the imagination of the spectator. I have made a film like *And the Ship Sails On,* in which a ship is sunk by cannon fire. Well, I made that film without sea, without sky, without ships, without cannon. I made it all up in Cinecittà. But the viewer had the impression that there was sea, sky, seagulls, ships, cannon and all the rest. And this is what I still mean by cinema.

The Seventieth Birthday:
January 20, 1990

COSTANZO COSTANTINI: *Today you are seventy. How do you feel?*

FEDERICO FELLINI: Resigned. Resigned to replying as best I can to the questions that such an occasion prompts in its amiable but inescapable way. As you see, I really look the part of an old man today: dressing gown, a woolen blanket from my waist down and my mind's a blank. Keep your distance—I wouldn't like to infect you. I don't mean with my being seventy, but with Chinese flu, which has decided to celebrate the day with a gift of fever and nausea.

Do you believe in astrology? Do you like your star sign? Do you think it has had an influence on your work?

Long ago, while reading in one of those little books on star signs about the characteristics of a Capricorn baby, I thought I recognized myself when it said: "The Capricorn is talented from the very moment of birth."

Jesus Christ, Joan of Arc, Madame Pompadour, Marlene Dietrich, Edgar Allan Poe, Pasteur and Martin Luther King were all born under the sign of Capricorn. Which of these do you feel you most resemble?

As a youth, there were two models of masculine beauty and charisma whom I wanted desperately to resemble. One was the stage actor Febo Mari, with his long, aristocratic neck, his curly hair, his eyes at once imperious and languid. The other was Edgar Allan Poe, whose amazing face with its deathly, feverish pallor redeemed every drunkard in the world. Which of them do I most resemble? Madame Pompadour.

How do you conceive and perceive time?
I don't have any impression of time passing. As always, everything seems to be happening in an eternal present of which the past is a part as well as the future. Anyway, that's how I imagine it. Without doubt, it is the conditioning of my profession that makes me see myself in the middle of a studio surrounded by real people and characters invented by me who are just as real: friends and strangers, fleeting encounters, creatures of my dreams and my imagination. I can't tell the difference between one decade and another, between a film I made in the fifties and the one I will make next.

Do you fear old age?
In *The Voice of the Moon* there is a character whom Paolo Villaggio has made so true, authentic and alive that it disturbs me every time I see the film. It makes me laugh, but above all it makes me scared, communicating the sense of cold, unease and anxiety that beings lost in an unreachable galaxy might feel. Old age, every old person in the world spies on him, follows him night and day even into his bed. They bend down over him, as he pretends to sleep, infecting him with their sickeningly foul breath.

Have you attained what is termed "the peace of the senses"?
Do you remember the face that Oliver Hardy makes when, confronted by the disasters perpetrated by Stanley, he tries to

fix the viewer with a calm, long look, silently inviting him to bear witness to calamities of such enormity? Behold, to this question I make exactly the same face.

Are you frightened of death?
What should I reply? Yes, no, it depends, I don't know, I don't remember—what kind of reply do you expect? The inextinguishable curiosity that makes us wake up every morning and accompanies us throughout our lives ought not to desert us at the moment of the most unknowable of experiences, at least let's hope not. We shall see.

Do you believe in immortality?
I have come to believe in it and would advise everyone to do likewise, if only as a form of mental hygiene. Belief in it stimulates and nourishes the imagination—even if the prospect of still being interviewed by you on my 7,000th birthday might cause me some perplexity.

Do you think about God? How do you imagine him?
Up until the age of five, I had no doubts: God looked like Count Gualtiero Ripa. He was our landlord. He was very thin, always dressed in blue—even his bowler hat was the color of heaven. He had a long white beard, which fell upon his chest and sometimes parted like a theater curtain to reveal an azure waistcoat with a sparkling gold fob chain. He would pass through the courtyard, silent and rapt in thought, never looking anyone in the face, with a cigar in a holder between his teeth. Once my mother said in a low voice, "And who does he think he is—God Almighty?" When I was older, the image of the grand old man in the Sistine Chapel replaced that of the Count in my imagination, and it survives even to this day.

Do you pray?

No longer in the way we used to as children, with our grand-mother, who would suddenly appear in the bedroom with a candlestick in her hand. The lighted candle would illuminate from below her beautiful face, like a Red Indian's. Pointing a long finger at us, she would ask, "Have you said your prayers?" Once she surprised my brother and me while we were chanting our prayers to the tune of "Titina." She threatened to set the guard dog free and put us in its place in the basket in the winter cold. But now I conceive of prayer not just as a formal act of devotion, but also as the technique of a secret, psycho-logical alchemy for obtaining miracles and wonders.

Do you think that you will remain creative into your nineties, like Titian, Picasso and De Chirico?

Yes. I have promised Berlusconi, poor man. I must always pro-vide him with more delicious opportunities to stuff my films with his million commercial breaks. On the subject, I have learned that Angelo Rizzoli junior has sold the films I made for his grandfather to Berlusconi for eternity—*I Vitelloni, La Dolce Vita* and *8½*—along with three or four others. My God, what can one do?

The Lifetime Achievement Oscar:
March 1993

COSTANZO COSTANTINI: *Are you pleased? You were acclaimed as never before; it was a triumph.*

FEDERICO FELLINI: It was a challenge to come to Los Angeles in my condition: my head spins, I sway and the cervical arthrosis gives me no respite. Added to the real discomfort is a kind of autosuggestion: the more I think that I'm going to fall, the more I feel like I'm falling—at least, so it seems to me. The rehearsal for the ceremony was very wearisome. Marcello, Sophia and I felt like novice actors. Beforehand, as a gesture of courtesy, I had gone to the headquarters of the Directors' Guild of America on Sunset Boulevard, where the newly created John Huston Prize was announced, but I didn't even go into the hall, because I wasn't steady on my feet.

But during the ceremony itself you seemed in fine form.
I made a great effort to seem in fine form and say those few words. What could I have said in such a brief amount of time, hardly thirty seconds? Even if I had been able, it wouldn't have been possible to say anything memorable, anything more than an expression of gratitude for my fifth Oscar. The Oscars are organized to perfection: obedient to the timing, the rhythms and the methods of the spectacle. It is a show within showbiz,

Fellini in the arms of Oscar.

dedicated to those who produce shows. Had my time not been so rigorously rationed, maybe I could have made a speech that was intelligent, spirited, pleasant, detached and emotional— Felliniesque, in a word. I could have overcome the fear of not corresponding to the image Americans have of me, both as a director and as a person. But the ceremony doesn't allow it. Everything is calculated like a film sequence.

But this fear wasn't evident in the slightest. On the contrary, you displayed great self-assurance.
If I had had to suggest to an actor or actress—Marcello Mastroianni or Sophia Loren, for example—how to carry themselves, what attitude to assume and what lines to say,

perhaps I would have been totally at ease. But in this instance it was me who was the actor, or the actor and director at the same time. Directing oneself isn't easy; it requires a split personality.

But you have already directed yourself in Intervista, *and have been an actor in Rossellini's* Miracle *and Mazursky's* Alex in Wonderland.
In front of the movie camera, not in front of an audience like that in the Dorothy Chandler Pavilion and all the world's cameramen.

But you directed yourself magnificently.
If I don't find any more work as a director, I can always be an actor.

Were you expecting Giulietta to cry?
It's always in the cards. She's an extremely emotional creature. "Stop crying," I said to her through intuition because she was too far from the stage for me to actually see her tears. I know her better than myself. We have been together for around half a century. The audience was moved. Giulietta is much more popular and better loved than me.

When you all arrived at the Pavilion, she really was pestered more than you and Mastroianni by the news photographers, reporters and cameramen.
Yes, I noticed. It was an amazing sight. I, the maker of *La Dolce Vita,* had never seen anything like it: more than two thousand news photographers and cameramen besieging the celebrities who passed along the gangway, the sky lit up like day with revolving floodlights and the beams of helicopters hovering at low level. But Giulietta was also marveled at inside the theater. The fervor that surrounded her recalled to me the

joy the public had shown her when we came to Los Angeles to receive the Oscar for *La Strada*. The cheers were above all for Giulietta-Gelsomina, whom many mistook for a little urchin, for a clown. As well as being a great actress, Giulietta is also a star, or, at least, she handles herself in public much better than I do. I always feel ill at ease when I have to take part in society events—gala evenings, premières, official ceremonies— whereas Giulietta is completely at ease with them. She has a season ticket for the opera and often appears on television, sometimes as an "ambassadress" for UNICEF.

But popularity and success also give you pleasure.
I've never denied it. Success is a great nourishment for all those, like directors and actors, who play to an audience. I like popularity, but I don't seek it. I'd much rather that my films be popular, not me. At one time directors were eclipsed by the great movie stars, but now that is no longer the case. Today the real stars are the creators of the films. In Giulietta's case, however, she is as popular as her films: *La Strada, Nights of Cabiria, Juliet of the Spirits* and *Ginger and Fred*. Popularity can sometimes be a nuisance, but it also has positive and pleasant aspects. One time Giulietta had her bag snatched in Via Margutta, along with her bracelet, rings and watch. But when the culprits found out who their victim had been, they left the stolen goods for us to retrieve in a bar in Trastevere, a working-class quarter of the old city. This incident is a little paradoxical—I realize that it would have been nicer if she hadn't been mugged in the first place, but that's how things are these days.

What are Giulietta's special qualities as an actress?
Giulietta has the lightness of a phantom, a dream, an idea. She possesses the movements, the mimic skills and the cadences of a clown. She has the looks of amazement and of dismay,

unexpected moments of joy and just as startling descents into the sadness of a clown. She has an authentic "clown-ness." Ever since we began to work together, she has corresponded fully to my ideas, my intentions, my tastes and to the way I conceive an actress. Her clownish talent seems to me the distinctive sign of a real vocation for stage art. Because of these talents, she was the ideal performer for a film like *La Strada,* a perfect Gelsomina.

But Giulietta says that when you were preparing La Strada *she dreamed that you would give her the face of Greta Garbo or Katharine Hepburn.*
Giulietta is a woman both simple and complex at the same time. She's a typical example of her star sign. All Pisceans have this double nature, this basic ambiguity. In the blink of an eye they change aspect, transform themselves, like mirrors that turn in on themselves. Giulietta is full of contradictions, ambivalences and contrasts. The characters of Gelsomina and Cabiria could not have been born without her; they would never have entered my mind if I hadn't had her as my model, although they came into being against her will. In one respect she was glad that I had chosen her to play the characters, but in another she was reluctant and made a bit of a fuss, as if she were unwilling to give expression to something dark and enigmatic within herself that she wanted to deny. Side by side with the Giulietta who said yes, there appeared another, who said no. The truth is that as an actress she wanted to be the opposite of those characters she embodied in my films.

Was she also opposed to Juliet of the Spirits?
Less so than for *La Strada* and *The Nights of Cabiria.* That's because she realized that I wanted to turn her into a different character from the other two. *Juliet of the Spirits* was inspired by her. I wanted to use the cinema as an instrument to capture

something of the transparency of reality and, in this respect, Giulietta seemed to me the most suitable guide. Giulietta is a surreal creature. The visionary, magical, enchanted aura found in some of my films issues from her. The character she played in *Juliet of the Spirits,* so ambiguous and changeable, is the one that most represents her, the one in which she is most identifiable and personified.

You yourself have admitted that on the set you sometimes treated her badly or, at least, were more demanding of her than of the other actors and actresses.
I made more demands on her because, given our relationship, I expected her to pick everything up at once, without my having to give her a lot of instructions. I've known Giulietta for years and life together has always been a source of continual observation. She never forgot and never forgets that she is my wife. On the set she behaves both like an actress and like my wife. In fact, she would persistently come on the set to find out if I felt cold, or had damp shoes, or wanted a cappuccino. Anyway, I recognize that I was sometimes unfair to her and too demanding.

Do you feel some sense of guilt?
Maybe so. Who doesn't feel pangs of guilt? The sense of guilt is innate in us Catholics. But my relationship with Giulietta has never changed, fundamentally. She is a mysterious being who can reflect, in her relationship with me, an agonizing nostalgia for innocence and perfection. More than once I have been tempted to say to her, "But were you really born and did you really grow up to be like you are? You weren't created this perfect creature?" I don't want to exaggerate or seem ridiculous, but for me Giulietta was a sort of Beatrice: sweet, radiant and ineffable.

On the other hand, has your relationship with Marcello Mastroianni—who presented you with the Lifetime Achievement Oscar—always been perfect?
In 1987, at the Venice Festival, it was I who presented him with the Lifetime Golden Lion, so now we are quits. Our relationship has never suffered any notable alterations. Ever since we made *La Dolce Vita* together, it has always been a friendly, faithful and affectionate association. He has always been a loyal and true friend. Our friendship has even survived unscathed those unpleasant incidents that occurred between us, perhaps against the wishes of us both, but that could have compromised it. In 1966 he didn't think twice about breaking his contract with the Teatro Sistina of Rome, where he was playing in *Ciao, Rudy.* He paid a penalty of 100 million lire so that he could play the lead role in *The Voyage of G. Mastorna,* the film that I never managed to make. I remember he said to me, "Don't worry, Federico, I'll wait." And he waited with infinite patience.

But you sought other actors to play the lead in the film?
Yes, because he was always committed to something else, but he was my ideal actor for the part. Ever since *8½,* it is no accident that he has been defined as my alter ego. Marcello was always touring the world. He's a deluxe tourist, as he calls himself. He preferred to accept films that weren't shot in Rome. I was one of the few directors for whom he was prepared to work in Rome. He needed to escape, to move to distant, remote countries. From time to time he would call me from the most exotic places.

Why did he need to escape?
Marcello runs away from himself, from the situations he himself has created. This is part of the psychology of the actor,

who is accustomed to giving life, on screen and stage, to other personalities, to dressing up and disguising himself. As well as being a very intelligent, sensitive and attentive person, Marcello immediately perceives situations and always satisfies one's high expectations. He is a perfect, exemplary actor, who always places himself completely at the disposal of the director.

So why didn't you see each other more often?
We mainly saw each other on the set or on trips abroad to promote our films. He was always with me on big occasions. As well as at Cannes for *La Dolce Vita,* he accompanied me to Moscow and New York for the awards for *8½.* At the Moscow Festival the film was part of the official program. Even Nikita Khrushchev attended the showing. I recall that during the performance he dozed off, or at least pretended to, perhaps so as not to compromise himself too much. The Central Committee of the Communist Party had warned the President of the International Jury, Grigorij Cuchraj, not to award a prize to *8½,* which was of course no kind of film for the proletariat. But Cuchraj, emboldened by the support of the foreign members of the jury, awarded it the prize all the same. Afterward he had to flee Moscow to escape the reprisals of the Soviet Communist Party. But Khrushchev had sympathy for him, seeing that he was to some extent the official representative of "the thaw."

Mastroianni describes these trips as a series of great adventures.
Indeed they were. Marcello would become as excited as a child about everything he saw, and was received everywhere with great warmth. In New York, while a season of my films was being presented at Lincoln Center, all the great American directors came to welcome us and congratulated Marcello more than me.

But weren't there other reasons why Mastroianni would quit Rome and escape from himself and the situations he had created? And wasn't there something you shared, some bond greater than the association between director and actor?

Just as I have with Giulietta, so Marcello has a profound relationship with his wife, Flora Carabella, by whom he has had a daughter, Barbara, who has worked with me as a set designer. I think he still feels the need of her as a companion; in fact I think she is his truest friend, a kind of secret and precious one.

But this mystic bond hasn't prevented him from having other relationships.

Marcello has succeeded in finding a miraculous balance between Flora and other women. He has never taken the step of breaking up his marriage, maybe because he feels protected by it. On the other hand, he finds it impossible to break his other emotional attachments. As he admits himself, it's always the women who leave him, because he cannot find the resolution to make a clean break with his past.

Flora says that Marcello is a great liar, an incurable fibber, just like you.

I can say that he has never lied to me, never uttered falsehoods. One has to examine the context. Marcello uses lies as diplomatic stratagems in order to spare others from suffering. He deserves a medal for his concern for others. He deserves an Oscar for the patience, the tenacity and the intelligence with which he has preserved his relationship with Flora.

Do you count on making other films with him?

Of course I would like to, especially to lighten the load of old age and make us feel younger. Sometimes I'm taken with the idea of another film at Fregene, even though it's some years since I last went there. A big adventure film, set in that thirties scenery: smugglers' boats, which plow the seas by night with their secret cargoes, bandits and criminals who hide in those sumptuous and crumbling villas, rich and beautiful women roaming the beach like phantoms, with Mastroianni in the role of a supercop who would make Philip Marlowe blench. But perhaps this is all an old man's fantasy.

Has the Lifetime Oscar not fired you up to begin a new film?
The Lifetime Oscar is particularly gratifying because it is an award for a director's complete *oeuvre,* freeing him from the invidious task of choosing between his films, always a difficult process. Without doubt, it is a stimulus to making other films, especially as it seems a good omen for the cyclical rebirth of the cinema. But at the same time it also seems like a conclusion, like an invitation to draw a line under my work and make way for younger talents.

But artists are long-lived, as you yourself have said many times. Titian completely changed his style of painting in his nineties; De Chirico painted into his nineties, Picasso until he was ninety-two and Chagall until he was ninety-eight.
I am flattered by these comparisons, but I doubt if my creative life will be as long as theirs. The one element in my favor is that I can never manage to draw up any kind of balance sheet, not even of a day's events. I admire and envy those who not only weigh their achievements, but also make new plans for the future, even for the third millennium. But I'm not even able to say what I'll be doing tomorrow.

And yet in your films you anticipated events.
I anticipated nothing. What happened was meant to happen, it was in the natural order of things. We are all subject to a kind of fateful predetermination.

The Death of Federico Fellini: October 1993

On June 29, 1993, the Italian Associated Press Agency announced:

> Federico Fellini is working in great secrecy at Cinecittà, with the art director Antonello Geleng and the costume designer Maleno Millenotti, on the preparation of *A Director's Notebook: The Actor.* Shooting will commence at the end of August and the film will be ready for April 1994. At this moment the director is developing the plot, which is constructed from memories, anecdotes and imaginary elements taken from his many years' professional experience and his relationships with actors. The film, which its maker has defined as "a declaration of love by a puppeteer for his fabulous creations," will star Paolo Villaggio and other actors associated with Fellini, including Marcello Mastroianni and Giulietta Masina.

But on June 29, 1993 Federico Fellini was not working in great secrecy at Cinecittà on *A Director's Notebook: The Actor.* He was at Zurich, where, on June 16, he had undergone an operation at the University Hospital that had taken longer than expected. He was released on June 28 and went to convalesce at the Dodler, a hotel in the upper part of the city.

For a while, Fellini had suffered from high blood pressure and arthritis, but neither had caused him great problems or prevented him from working. Things first took a serious turn in September 1992, when he suffered an aortic aneurysm of the abdomen. He became very worried about his condition at the time, but managed to conceal it beneath the ironic, and self-ironic, sense of humor that never deserted him. He had started to consult one doctor after another. He wanted to be sure whether it was a really serious illness and, especially, if he should have an operation, or not. According to his own account, half the doctors advised him to have surgery, the other half told him he could continue safely as he was. Among the latter was even Professor Paolo Pola, head of the Angiology

Sets by Antonello Geleng for Fellini: A Director's Notebook, *the television movie Fellini was working on until the beginning of 1993.*

Sets by Antonello Geleng for Fellini: A Director's Notebook, *the television movie Fellini was working on until the beginning of 1993.*

Department of the Columbus Hospital in Rome. He sided with those who advised Fellini against surgery, but Fellini was haunted by the thought of the risks he ran by not having an operation.

On March 15, 1993, I accompanied Fellini to a medical center in Rome that specialized in the care of arthrosis problems, a kind of chiropractor's. It was in Piazza della Libertà, about a hundred meters from Via Margutta. We met at Canova's, the bar in Piazza del Popolo, and went to the clinic on foot, although Fellini would have preferred to take a taxi. I had been present when Professor Silvano Silvij had visited him. "What illnesses have you had or do you have?" he had asked. "I have an aortic aneurism of the abdomen," Fellini had answered, but without betraying the least anxiety, as if he had told him he had a cold. So Silvij had sent him to the French chiropractor Hervé Granet. He attended Granet's clinic for four days. Later the doctor reported, "He has chronic cervical arthrosis, which gives him a stoop and sometimes causes him headaches and dizziness. But it's fairly normal in a man of seventy-three. I prescribed for him a therapy of manipulations and tractions for four days. He had great faith in the cure, but afterward I never saw him again."

On March 26, 1993, Fellini flew to Los Angeles with Giulietta and Mastroianni to receive the Lifetime Oscar. Both during the journey and during his stay in Los Angeles, he complained of pains in his upper spine and dizzy spells. A doctor was called, who visited him in his apartment in the Beverly Hilton. On learning of the aortic aneurism, the doctor had told him, "In such cases, we Americans operate." On his return to Rome, Fellini began to think seriously about surgery, especially because he wanted to make a start on *A Director's Notebook: The Actor,* a film that had been postponed several times. The producer, Leo Pescarolo, had already concluded an international agreement and had presold the film in Germany and Great Britain.

By May 1993, Fellini decided to have the operation. Accompanied by one of his family doctors, Professor Turchetti, he traveled to Zurich to consult Professor Marko Turina, head of the Cardiovascular Surgery Department of the University Hospital. After a series of examinations and tests, Professor Turina made it clear to him that the operation was now absolutely necessary, even though his condition was not yet critical.

On June 12, Fellini returned to Zurich for the operation. He was accompanied by Giulietta and Simona Tavanti, the daughter of Giulietta's sister, Eugenia. They took rooms at the Hotel Europe, near University Hospital.

Angelo Arpa, the Jesuit priest who had been a friend of the director's since the fifties and who had dared to defend *La Dolce Vita* from the attacks of the Vatican, recounts, "On June 11, Federico wanted to see me. We met at Canova's. He was very calm. He said to me, 'It's an operation that doesn't present any problems.' "

However, the operation met with enormous problems. Simona Tavanti relates:

Turchetti did not come with us because he had faith in the surgeons who would perform the operation. Turina and his assistant, Professor Michele Genoni. Federico entered the hospital on June 14 and was operated on on June 16. He was taken into the theater at seven-thirty in the morning. At midday he was taken back to his room. He woke up from the anesthesia. It appeared that all had gone well. But some time later Federico suffered a hemorrhage and was taken to the resuscitation room. At half past one he was given more anesthetic and underwent a second operation. At seven o'clock in the evening, Professor Genoni told us there had been an embolism. Federico was taken back to his room late in the morning of the seventeenth. He slept for two whole days. He awoke on the nineteenth, a Saturday. On his bedside table was a note. He had written it on the evening of June 15. It was addressed to Giulietta. He had told her that he loved her, that it had been a great joy to have her by his side at those times, and that he would be glad to see her face again when he came out of the anesthetic. But it was quite difficult waking him up again. During his sleep he called out his mother's name.

Toward the end of July, Fellini left Zurich and moved to the Grand Hotel in Rimini to continue his convalescence. But on August 3 he suffered a stroke, which for a while caused his family and friends great anxiety. Having recovered from the stroke, Fellini was taken to Ferrara on August 20 to begin rehabilitative therapy at the famous Ospedale San Giorgio. On September 18, he made a lightning visit to Rome to meet Giulietta, who was recovering from an unknown complaint at the Columbus Clinic. On October 9 he was brought back to Rome to continue his rehabilitative therapy at the Neurological Clinic of the Policlinico Umberto I, in anticipation of a speedy return to his home and his work.

After his first night, Fellini had asked Rinaldino Geleng to come and sleep in his room, because he was frightened of spending the night alone. Geleng had accepted willingly and from October 10 had shared a room with the director on the first floor of the Neurological Clinic. Geleng gives a graphic firsthand account of Fellini's state of mind and his surroundings:

Fellini suffered from insomnia and was increasingly subject to attacks of anxiety and depression. Thanks to the tranquilizers and sedatives he received, he would fall asleep, but after half or three-quarters of an hour, he would wake up again suddenly, tossing and turning with worry, and would lapse again into a state of depression and anguish. To tell the truth, Fellini didn't want to stay at the Policlinico. He wanted to go back home to Via Margutta, to be with Giulietta. "But what am I doing here?" he would ask me insistently. Every night he would ask me once or twice: "Rinaldino, please dress me and take me back home." These words will resound within me for the rest of my life. Every night, and I mean every night, he would have a choking fit. Then he would beg me to call the doctor on duty to bring him the oxygen mask. But the doctor would usually be busy with patients in even worse condition than Fellini. I would ring and ring, but the doctor wouldn't come. Three, five, ten minutes went by, but for Fellini they were an eternity. One night, the oxygen mask didn't arrive for fifteen minutes. When the doctor finally arrived, Fellini would calm down a little and feel somewhat safer. He would do everything to detain the doctor in his room as long as possible, telling him the history of his illness, even if he had already told him before, and resorting to other expedients. But the doctor could never stay long with him.

Fellini said to me, "I thought I would be taken home; it's absurd to be brought back from Ferrara to Rome and not to be taken back to my house and Giulietta." He pronounced these words with a suppressed sadness, making every effort to hold back the tears. But from time to time, he would burst out crying and wail, "Giulietta! Giulietta!"

The nursing staff, like the doctors on duty, did everything possible for him as well as for the other patients. They were heroes. But during the night there were never enough of them for all those sick people, many of whom were afflicted with nervous and mental disorders. The staff would move from one room to the next without respite, without a chance to catch their breath but with infinite patience, helping those in greatest need. Desperate cries for help would be heard. One night, after I had rung for ten minutes, I decided to leave our room. But I found myself confronted with a repulsive sight: two nurses up to their elbows in patients' excrement. The atmosphere of the place was full of anguish and torment and ended up making me depressed also.

Sometimes Fellini could not even go to the lavatory. He

was not fond of the bedpan, preferring to seat himself upon the commode, that contraption made famous by the Sun King. But since the nursing staff were slow to arrive, he was forced to hold on, and return to his bed. "After that I'll need an enema," he said to me once in resignation. In an attempt to console him, I said, "Federico, we're not at Cinecittà now, where you can have everything. You would ask for a hydrofoil, and they would get you a hydrofoil; you would ask for a tempestuous sea, as in *And the Ship Sails On,* and in no time you would have one. Now we're at the Policlinico." He would appear to calm down, but later he would again start to ask for something, especially the oxygen mask.

This nightmare would be prolonged interminably. To put an end to it as soon as possible, Fellini would ask me to dress him around five or six o'clock in the morning and to call the nurses to take him up to the next floor for his rehabilitative exercises, although he knew full well that at that hour the so-called motor reeducation service for neurological problems was closed. To distract him, I used to remind him of our youthful exploits, when in Rome we would go into restaurants and hotels without the money to pay the bill. I would put before his eyes the photos of Valeria Marini, the well-endowed soubrette who was all the rage on television. If he was in the mood, he would say to me: "Rinaldino, get the sketch pad and hold it for me," and he would start to draw, jotting down little sketches. Then I said, "I see you're still in form. You'll be like Michelangelo, who was still drawing and making sculptures at eighty-nine." "Michelangelo was Michelangelo," he objected. "Don't lose heart, Federico," I said to him, and to make him laugh I reminded him of the story of the little boy who, as he passed St. Peter's, said to Michelangelo, "Hey, Michelà, the Pope says that if you don't get on with it, he's going to use wallpaper in the Sistine Chapel instead!"

Toward the end he was seized with nostalgia for Rimini; he wanted to buy himself a house by the harbor, and I talked to him in Romagnolo.

Around October 15 or 16, Giulietta decided to send a private nurse to him, who would attend him in his moments of need without having to call the nursing staff. I remember he said to the nurse, "Sit there and don't move," indicating a corner of the room. After the arrival of the private nurse, he was calmer and nicer to everyone. He gave nicknames to the doctors and nursing staff, as he used to with the members of his crew and his actors and actresses. One doctor, who was a little shorter than the others, he nicknamed "the little sacristan"; one nurse, who was more attractive than the others, he named "the super-Titianesque." All the medical staff called him Federi and treated him with great admiration and affection, but only when they got the chance and didn't have to tend to the disturbed patients who cried and roared and howled.

However, in the late afternoon of October 17, Fellini, while he was eating his dinner, was seized with a choking fit. At that moment, Enzo Da Castro, his production secretary, and Roberto Mannoni, his production director, were by his side. Enzo Da Castro recounts:

At a quarter to six or thereabouts a male nurse had brought him his dinner on a tray and had left the room. The tray contained a bowl of light soup, some pieces of cheese, an individual portion of mozzarella and some stewed fruit, each article wrapped in aluminum foil. I unwrapped the foil and helped Fellini to sit up in bed, putting some pillows behind his back. First he ate the soup, then one piece of cheese. Between mouthfuls, he joked with us while I cut up his bread for him. With his fork he cut his mozzarella in two and ate one of the halves; then he put the other in his mouth and swallowed it. But all at once he froze; he turned pale, bluish and ashen. He felt himself suffocating. He couldn't breathe and was about to choke to death. Then I raised him a little higher in his bed, making him sit up straight. With my left hand I took hold of his head, and with my right hand I slapped his back, saying to him, "Federico, spit, spit!" But he couldn't manage to expel the piece of mozzarella. A suction tube might have helped, but where would I find one? Federico was turning paler and paler, his head was cold as ice. Powerless to help him, I felt as if a dagger was entering my heart as I watched him suffocating like this.

Roberto Mannoni said, "I immediately felt his pulse: it no longer gave signs of life. I began to cry out for help. Two young male nurses and a woman, who was the doctor on duty, rushed in. "Cardiac arrest! Cardiac arrest!" the woman doctor said, and began to give him heart massage, asking us to leave the room. De Castro adds, "I telephoned Professor Turchetti, the doctor in charge of Fellini, and told him, 'Fellini is choking to death. Come, come immediately!' We had no idea how things stood in Fellini's room, whether or not the heart massage had worked and Fellini had recovered. We were in a state of dreadful anxiety. After some fifteen minutes, another doctor arrived. He was the resuscitator; he carried with him a box of professional instruments. Right afterward Turchetti arrived. But by now our hopes for Fellini's recovery were minimal. For a person who cannot breathe, fifteen minutes are like a century. Had Mannoni and I not been present, who could have helped Fellini, unable as he was to speak, to cry out or to ask for help? In all probability, he would have died without anyone realizing. . . . Around six-thirty Fellini was taken away. He had tubes in his nose. They took him to the Anesthesiology and Resuscitation Institute of the Policlinico, which was several hundred meters away."

Fellini had lapsed into a coma and never recovered consciousness. It lasted until October 31, when, at noon, he died.

"The cinema has lost a genius," announced television and radio

Notes for a film written by Fellini while in the clinic in October 1993.
The figure with the violin is a self-portrait.

newscasters throughout the world. Every cinematographic production in the world stopped immediately, observing several minutes
of silence in honor of the departed Maestro. At the Policlinico and
in Via Margutta, hundreds and hundreds of messages of condo-
lence arrived from directors, actors, writers, heads of government,
heads of state and ordinary people. The message from Boris Yeltsin
and his wife, Naina, read, "The name of the excellent Maestro of
cinematographic art will always have its place in the history of world
culture."

The newspapers of November 1 vied with each other in paying
tribute to the dead man, with front-page articles and huge headlines. The *Times:* "He was one of the very few directors who have

renewed the cinema of the post-war period"; the *New York Times:* "The world which Fellini presents us, albeit constructed in studios, reveals the true essence of the external world: a circus"; *Frankfurter Zeitung:* "He was the greatest creator of myths in European cinema"; *Libération:* "Maestro of the Cinema, Italy loses her great poet."

On November 1, Fellini's body, dressed in the dinner suit he had worn at the Oscar ceremony, was displayed at Cinecittà in Studio No. 5, the legendary location for the majority of his masterpieces. The coffin, surmounted by a corona of white flowers and guarded by *carabinieri* in full dress, had for its background an enormous panel, which portrayed a blue sky in evocation of "The Infinite." An immense crowd paid their tributes to the corpse in a profound silence broken only by the music of Nino Rota and Nicola Piovani, writers of the soundtracks of Fellini's films.

The funeral service took place on November 2 in the Basilica of Santa Maria of the Angels. Cardinal Silvestrini officiated:

> The final image Fellini leaves us, he who was a master of images, is that of himself immobile and speechless in the shadow of a prolonged agony. From this agony he has now departed in search of Our Lord to ask Him—like Nicodemus in the Gospel according to St. John—how it is possible for a man to be born again when he is old? In the Gospel Our Lord said to Nicodemus, "Marvel not that I said unto thee, Ye must be born again. The wind bloweth where it listeth, and thou hearest the sound thereof, but canst not tell whence it cometh, and whither it goeth." Federico knew that this wind exists. He heard its mysterious sounds. This wind was his own poetic force, which made him able to transfigure people and things.

"I want to go with him," said Giulietta Masina in a murmur when the coffin was placed in the hearse that would take it to Rimini. But the actress, who was ill with cancer, survived him, in increasing pain, for some five months. She died on March 23, 1994.

Coda: Reflections on Art, Life and the Cinema

COSTANZO COSTANTINI: *What is an artist for you?*
FEDERICO FELLINI: For me, the artist is someone who is called by demons and must reply to this summons. Doing so he is cast into a kind of galaxy with which he has special, arcane relationships. The problem is to recognize the sounds, the colors, the signs that correspond to the voice that called him. Once this problem is resolved, he need do nothing except perform in extrasensory fashion. When I enter into this state of grace, it is not I who directs the film, but the film that directs me. A huge amount of sensitivity is always required: you have entered a city you don't know but in which you must move with the lightness of a vampire, without ideas, ideologies, preconceptions, if not without everything. This is like the prologue, the atrium, the anteroom of creativity; only afterward do your practical experience, your craftsmanship and professionalism come in; in other words, the hard work of making creativity materialize. An artist does not do what he wants, but what he can: this tension is what constitutes art.

Do you regard cinema as an art form?
Yes and no. It is an art form and at the same time a circus, a funfair, a voyage aboard a kind of "ship of fools," an adventure,

an illusion, a mirage. It's an art form that has nothing to do with the other arts, least of all with literature. It's an autonomous art form. If at all, it's related to painting through its treatment of light. The heart of every object, both in cinema and in painting, is light. In cinema the light comes before the subject, the plot, the characters: it is light that expresses what the director means. Some critic in an attempt to belittle me has written that I am a "pictorial" director, but actually he couldn't have said anything more flattering. It's no surprise I have a profound sympathy with the painter; I envy him. The great painter is happy, serene, long-lived, more privileged than a poet. He's respected by women and friends; and if he could be respected a little more by the tax inspectors, he would be extraordinarily fortunate.

What painters do you admire the most?
I've always been fond of certain Italian painters: Scipione, Mafai, Rosai, Campigli, Carrà, Sironi and De Chirico. It's incredible that it really was only during the Fascist years that Italian painting attained its highest expression. Sironi is a great painter who is still not fully appreciated. For someone like me who makes films, De Chirico's metaphysical painting is extraordinary: he has invented Italy, with her piazzas, her streets, her colonnades, her seascapes; an Italy at once realistic and poetic. But the artist I admire the most, to the extent that I have dreamed about his work many times, is Picasso. For me he is the symbol, the archetype, the demiurge of creativity. I've dreamed about him four times, always in moments of crisis. One time I dreamed that I found myself in a menacing, emerald-green sea under a stormy sky when I noticed someone swimming in front of me with vigorous strokes. All at once he turned around and I saw that it was Picasso. That dream has stayed with me a long time, like the echo of a note. Another time, I remember that I was struggling with the opening of

The Voyage of G. Mastorna and I dreamed that I was in Picasso's house: the artist was in the kitchen and talked to me nonstop all through the night. When I awoke I felt myself bathed in a horizon of light. Why did I dream of Picasso? Because he is the artist with whom I would most like to identify myself. At the time of those dreams I viewed his pictures with a certain distance and diffidence, due to ignorance. But now, every time I see them I immediately feel a kind of complicity; I'm completely seized and shaken by them, by their richness and force, their life. Picasso is a painter who is totally, absolutely free. But, paradoxically, I think that total liberty is dangerous for an artist, in the sense that he might use it not to create, but to squander his artistic talent. In my opinion, you have to have some sort of tyranny. I would be in favor of an abstract state authority which ordered me to create images constantly. The Popes, who well understood the infantile psychology of artists, would summon them and command them to paint.

Are you happy with your relationships with women?
I've succeeded in reaching a mutual understanding with Giulietta. I don't feel oppressed, mutilated, crushed. I have no need of a divorce. If I think about the divorce referendum, I'm overcome with a sense of shame; I feel I'm living in an absurd country. I can't quite understand how this question gets in the way of everything else; the referendum has turned into a search for the Absolute. We've reached a grotesque point. It's marriage that should be abolished. The law should say: "Thou shalt not marry." Or the marriage should be renewable each year, like a driving license. To constrain two people who don't know each other, and neither of whom knows themselves, to live together for a lifetime is like shutting up two newborn infants in a box and forcing them to grow up together, each with his feet in the other's mouth. Two terrible and hideous monsters would be the outcome.

What do you think about relations between men and women in Italy?

We must regard the situation of Italian women with shame. There is a horrendous sexism against women by men. But women are also confused. The equality between men and women is a blasphemy against biology. I don't know how it started, this physical superiority of men and subjugation of women, or how we reached this state: but I have to say that even the best of us men are either erotomaniacs or feeble aesthetes. I don't know what a woman really is. In women I always see myself, in the sense that I project onto them my own desires. Woman represents what we don't possess, but since we don't know what we don't possess, we project onto them our own ignorance. Jung says that the woman is placed just where our darkness begins. Since the Italian male, through the influence of the Catholic Church, has remained a child, and since it is he of the two sexes who knows himself the least, he projects onto the woman an immense ignorance.

You have a keen interest in Jung. Have you derived benefit from reading his texts, from psychology and psychoanalysis?

Psychology has always fascinated me. Of all the sciences, it is for me the foremost, the fundamental starting point. It should be taught from nursery school. I'm a friend of Ernest Bernhard, the Jungian psychoanalyst, who has been a great aid in helping me to understand Jungian psychology. It was he who made me grasp that our dream life is no less important than our waking life, especially for the artist. It's owing to him that I am more receptive to Jung's ideas, that clairvoyant scientist whom everybody should read. I was greatly sustained by reading Jung. Contrary to what has been said, I have never been in analysis, but I do believe in psychoanalysis. In Italy people don't even know what it is; they reject it with the same superficiality and condescension that characterizes everything. It's ridiculous not to believe in psychoanalysis. It's like not believing in chemistry or mathematics. Today everything is for commercial ends, even psychoanalysis. Psychoanalysis permits us to establish a more profound view of our lives; it helps us to free ourselves from taboos; it enlarges our consciousness. It asks us to look at ourselves in a mirror to see our desires, even unpleasant ones, but at least recognized as our own. But today psychoanalysts throw you out as soon as you have paid the bill, even if you have tears in your eyes, because punctual payment helps the patient to recovery. Even politicians would benefit from psychoanalysis. The Italian is very ignorant and would avail himself of any discipline, but the Church has kept us in a kind of eternal darkness, ignorant of any possible truth. A science that aims to let man know himself is indispensable in a society based on ignorance and conformism.

The British Film Institute has published in Sight and Sound *the league table of the ten best films in the history of cinema in the judgment of major international directors. In third and fourth place are* 8½ *and* La Strada. *Are you pleased?*
As far as it concerns myself, I can express only the greatest satisfaction. But I don't know what the other eight films are and so can't say anything more about it.

I will tell you what they are. In first place is Citizen Kane *by Orson Welles. Are you in agreement?*
Absolutely, but I must put something on record. These league tables are drawn up periodically. Usually we are asked what are the ten films in the history of cinema that might save us from some hypothetical catastrophe. Wouldn't it be more accurate to say which ones might save us from television? In any case, it is hard to answer these questions. The best, in absolute terms? How can one say? A film, a book, a concert can please you because you are in a certain state of mind. You see a film

at a certain point in your life, or at a certain time of day, in one city rather than another, seated next to someone, known or unknown, who nevertheless enhances your enjoyment and appreciation of the performance.

You say you agree about Citizen Kane. *Why?*
Citizen Kane, which Orson Welles made and starred in when he was twenty-five years old in 1941, is the first "different" film to appear in America in the thirties and forties. American cinema of the period was extraordinarily advanced, but apart from Charlie Chaplin and John Ford, directors refrained from advertising and imposing themselves as auteurs. They were making good, even great, films, but they privileged the status of the actors, the stars, putting them before themselves. American cinema was symbolized by Chaplin and Garbo, for me more by Chaplin than Garbo, because of the love I have always had for comic actors like Buster Keaton, Harold Lloyd, the Marx Brothers, and Laurel and Hardy.

In what sense was Citizen Kane *a "different" film?*
In every sense. It was the expression of an auteur, a creator, whose own appearance in that context had a striking effect. Indeed, it was other directors who first recognized that behind the images of *Citizen Kane* there was an auteur, or genius, who even put ceilings in the frame; who by the use of deep focus and wide angles picked out the background with the same sharpness as the foreground, in an immense depth of field. Besides the thematic interest, which is enormous in itself, *Citizen Kane* marks a revolution in the method of cinematographic narration. I have never seen the film again, but I'm sure it has preserved its extraordinary expressive power.

Didn't even Josef von Sternberg, the director of The Blue Angel, *impose himself as an auteur?*

The Blue Angel is one of the many instances where the female star takes precedence over the director. Indeed, the film would deserve a place in the list for the performances alone: the amazing, grotesque clown figure of Professor Unrad and the extraordinary feline quality of Marlene Dietrich as one of the most bewitching enchantresses in the history of cinema.

Turning to the other films. In second place is Scorsese's Raging Bull.

Martin Scorsese is a director, or auteur, of great talent, whom I first started to appreciate when I saw *Taxi Driver* and who has grown in my esteem with his subsequent films. My attraction to him grew immensely when I got to know him in person. He is a man who loves the cinema with a deep and infectious passion, and we can only look forward to even greater and more interesting films from him.

What do you think of Jean Vigo and L'Atalante, *the film that appears in fourth place?*

I have never seen *L'Atalante* and I feel a sense of shame in admitting it, even though I'm notorious for not spending my evenings in the cinema. But Jean Vigo is a great director.

Doesn't it strike you as strange that Chaplin's Modern Times *is considered on a par with Coppola's* The Godfather *and Hitchcock's* Psycho, *all three placed in fifth place?*

Charlie Chaplin: the very mention of the name prompts me to show my admiration, enthusiasm and gratitude. But *Modern Times* isn't the film of his I like the best. In place of *Modern Times* I would have substituted *City Lights* or *Monsieur Verdoux,* if it weren't that the final lecture Chaplin puts into the mouth of the protagonist sounds a little like electioneering. And so, *City Lights* it has to be: an art nouveau film, beautiful, sad and sweet, like the funeral monuments in the cemetery of Staglieno.

Like you, Coppola appears twice in the list: tied for fifth with The Godfather *and in ninth place with* The Godfather, Part II, *after Kurosawa's* The Seven Samurai *and Dreyer's* The Passion of Joan of Arc, *and before Kurosawa's* Rashomon. *What do you think of these choices?*
The Seven Samurai and *Rashomon,* as well as *The Passion of Joan of Arc,* would all have merited being put in first place. Dreyer and Kurosawa are geniuses. I couldn't say if I prefer *The Seven Samurai* or *Rashomon,* probably the latter, but they are both the work of a great director. Seeing these films is like reading Ariosto. I've seen something of all Coppola's films: *The Conversation, Apocalypse Now,* as well as *The Godfather* and *The Godfather, Part II.* He is a true storyteller: robust, red-blooded and powerful. He also has the courage to change genres, styles and taste, putting his talent at the service of the most disparate themes. As for Hitchcock, I prefer *The Birds* to *Psycho:* it is a clear-sighted, disturbing, mysterious and harsh psychoanalytic fable.

But you haven't said if Raging Bull, The Godfather, The God-father, Part II *and* Psycho *deserve their places in the list.*
I'm not saying they don't deserve them, but I would have included many other films and many other filmmakers. This is why I can't express a precise judgment on the subject.

What other films and which other directors would you have included?
One of Greta Garbo's films, *Stagecoach* by John Ford, Rossellini's *Paisà, The Discreet Charm of the Bourgeoisie* by Buñuel, *The Face* or *Wild Strawberries* by Bergman, Kubrick's *Barry Lyndon,* and perhaps a Laurel and Hardy film. *Stagecoach* is

cinema in its purest form, grandiose and spectacular. When I met John Ford, I tried to convey to him all my enthusiasm for the film and called it *Red Shadow,* translating directly from the Italian title. "Ah, what a nice title!" John said, with his black eye-patch, "but I never thought it up." *The Discreet Charm of the Bourgeoisie* is Buñuel at his most enigmatic, a filmmaker of genius. I might say that Buñuel is the greatest filmmaker of all because he brings off something no one else could manage: he makes cinema express itself through its own peculiar authentic and precious language—the language of dreams. In his films Buñuel dreams on our behalf, the audience's. But how could one draw up a list like this without including at least one Bergman film? Personally, of the two I mentioned, I prefer *The Face,* but the directors who were consulted ought to have put at least one of the great Swede's films on the list. And why not include one of the early Bond films, which represent cinema in its most direct and explicit essentials: adventure, an invincible and handsome hero, exotic locations, and beautiful women fainting with desire. That's not the only reason I cite Bond films, but also because I believe them to be the most reliable and serious document of the times in which we live: this continual blurring of the border between political activity and police activity, the ferocity of power struggles, insectlike in their ruthlessness. They anticipated everything we have read in the papers or seen on TV: assassination attempts, massacres, outrageous blackmail, spies everywhere, perhaps even in the porter's lodge of your own apartment house.

You haven't said why you would have put Kubrick's Barry Lyndon *on the list.*
Barry Lyndon is a film that produces in us the same kind of emotion that we feel in the presence of the great masterpieces of art and literature. Kubrick is a superb filmmaker. He possesses a great visionary genius, allied to the ability to translate

into powerful images his natural gift of prodigious imagination. Besides which, he has a talent I envy, one that many other American directors possess, such as Scorsese, Coppola and Altman, just to mention a few.

What is this talent?
They are ready to handle the most diverse themes without ever identifying themselves with one type of worldview or mode of expression, and yet always remaining recognizable by their style.

What explains this diversity of theirs in comparison with Italian directors?
The system. In America the production chooses a story, entrusts it to good writers and then proposes it to the director, who is thereby free from the risk of repeating himself, of always presenting the same persona.

Are you trying to criticize yourself?
I have declared countless times that I would like a patron who would oblige me to make this or that film, making use of my experience only as a director and freeing me from the risk of reflecting my own image. But I don't know if this will ever happen.

Fellini Filmography

1950   *Variety Lights (Luci del Varietà)*
CODIRECTOR: Alberto Lattuada
PRODUCERS: Federico Fellini, Alberto Lattuada (Capitolium Film)
SCREENPLAY: Alberto Lattuada, Federico Fellini, Tullio Pinelli, Ennio Flaiano
PHOTOGRAPHY: Otello Martelli
MUSIC: Felice Lattuada
DESIGN: Aldo Buzzi
EDITOR: Mario Bonotti
LEAD ACTORS: Peppino De Filippo, Carla Del Poggio, Giulietta Masina
This relentless and humorous chronicle of the fortunes of a fading variety artist who betrays his lover and his troupe for the attractions of a beautiful, talentless girl cynically on the make nevertheless retains a passionate tenderness toward the worlds in which Fellini learned his profession.

1952   *The White Sheik (Lo Sceicco bianco)*
PRODUCER: Luigi Rovere (PDG-OFI)
SCREENPLAY: Federico Fellini, Tullio Pinelli, Ennio Flaiano
PHOTOGRAPHY: Arturo Gallea

MUSIC: Nino Rota
DESIGN: Raffaele Tolfo
EDITOR: Rolando Benedetti
LEAD ACTORS: Brunella Bovo, Leopoldo Trieste, Alberto Sordi, Giulietta Masina

A classic Italian comedy of situation and character, in which the outward appearance of respectability and contentedness of a newlywed couple is demolished by the dreams and aspirations of the wife. This allows Fellini lovingly to satirize the chasm that separates reality and desire without avoiding the pain involved, and to record on film the world of the photographed cartoon-strip adventure and romance that has always been so much a part of Italian culture. Now celebrated, it was ignored when first presented at Venice.

1953   *I Vitelloni (Spivs, The Young and the Passionate)*
PRODUCER: Lorenzo Pegoraro (Peg Film, Rome, Cité Film, Paris)
SCREENPLAY: Federico Fellini, Tullio Pinelli, Ennio Flaiano
PHOTOGRAPHY: Otello Matrelli
MUSIC: Nino Rota
DESIGN: Mario Chiari
EDITOR: Rolando Benedetti
LEAD ACTORS: Franco Interlenghi, Franco Fabrizi, Alberto Sordi, Leopoldo Trieste, Riccardo Fellini, Leonora Ruffo, Lida Baarova

I Vitelloni recounts the aimless lives of five youths in Fellini's hometown of Rimini, this time viewing more severely their inability and responsibility, and their consequent shallowness. The balance of critique and compassionate tenderness in Fellini's treatment of the world he depicts earned the film immediate and unanimous respect. He was later to separate out the elements of the blend.

Un'Agenzia matromoniale (A Marriage Agency),
fourth episode of Amore in Città
PRODUCERS: Cesare Zavattini, Riccardo Ghione, Marco Fer-
reri (Faro Film)
SCREENPLAY: Federico Fellini, Tullio Pinelli
PHOTOGRAPHY: Gianni Di Venanzo
MUSIC: Mario Nascimbene
DESIGN: Gianni Polidori
EDITOR: Eraldo Da Roma
LEAD ACTORS: Antonio Cifariello, Livia Venturelli
Cesare Zavattini was aiming for cinematic journalism, stories
taken from reality. Fellini viciously subverts the genre, showing
how the search for the truth about a gentle, innocent girl on
the part of a reporter is a cruel exploitation of her feelings.

1954   *La Strada*
PRODUCERS: Dino De Laurentiis, Carlo Ponti (Produzione
Ponti-De Laurentiis)
SCREENPLAY: Federico Fellini, Tullio Pinelli, Ennio Flaiano
PHOTOGRAPHY: Otello Matrelli
MUSIC: Nino Rota
DESIGN: Mario Ravasco
EDITOR: Leo Catozzo
LEAD ACTORS: Giulietta Masina, Anthony Quinn, Richard
Basehart
A character endowed with divine grace, candid and angelic, is
pushed up against the most cruel and insensitive reality Fellini
can depict. But her suffering serves to redeem the man who
brutalizes her. This situation has been developing in all Fellini's
films up to this one. In *La Strada* it is pared down to its
essentials and illustrated through a wealth of subtly deployed
Christian, pagan and popular iconography. This is the first film
fully to display the power and lyricism of Fellini's vision, but
it paradoxically does so through the basest, most elemental

means, which led to its being considered as on the outer fringe of neorealism.

1955   *Il Bidone (The Swindle)*

PRODUCTION: Titanus (Rome), SGG (Paris)
SCREENPLAY: Federico Fellini, Tullio Pinella, Ennio Flaiano
PHOTOGRAPHY: Otello Martelli
MUSIC: Nino Rota
DESIGN: Dario Cecchi
EDITORS: Mario Serandrei, Giuseppe Vari
LEAD ACTORS: Broderick Crawford, Richard Basehart, Franco Fabrizi, Giulietta Masina, Lorella De Luca

A small-time con man's shallow opportunism leads to his eventual abandonment by all around him to a solitary death. But this man lives through a gradually intensifying hell of remorse all the while. Here the figurations of outward corruption and inner spiritual grace are held in a single character and left unresolved, perfectly embodying that blend of compassion and condemnation, with the possibility of redemption, that characterizes this phase of Fellini's output.

1957   *The Nights of Cabiria (Le Notti di Cabiria)*

PRODUCER: Dino De Laurentiis (Dino De Laurentiis, Rome, Les Films Marceau, Paris)
SCREENPLAY: Federico Fellini, Tullio Pinella, Ennio Flaiano, Pier Paolo Pasolini (dialogue)
PHOTOGRAPHY: Aldo Tonti, Otello Martelli
MUSIC: Nino Rota
DESIGN: Piero Gherardi
EDITOR: Leo Catozzo
LEAD ACTORS: Giulietta Masina, Amedeo Nazzari

Cairia is a resourceful, unrepentant prostitute who yearns nevertheless for love. But her desires and dreams are continually exploited and crushed by cruel reality, as became the rule in

Fellini's films of the fifties. As in *La Strada,* Giulietta Masina embodies an irrepressible vitality and a spiritual purity that nothing can destroy. *Le notti di Cabiria* concludes a trilogy of films of redemption that use characters at the lowest level of society to express a spiritual vision of inner humanity that is never explicitly Christian, but that leaves that interpretation very much open.

1960   *La Dolce Vita*

PRODUCER: Giuseppe Amato (Riama Fil, Rome, Pathé Consortium Cinéma, Paris)

SCREENPLAY: Federico Fellini, Tullio Pinelli, Ennio Flaiano, Brunello Rondi

PHOTOGRAPHY: Otello Martelli

MUSIC: Nino Rota

DESIGN: Piero Gherardi

EDITOR: Leo Catozzo

LEAD ACTORS: Marcello Mastroianni, Anouk Aimée, Anita Ekberg, Lex Barker, Yvonne Furneaux

Disillusion comes to the fore in an infernal journey through Roman high-life on the Via Veneto. Neither art nor culture, sex nor religion can bestow meaning on life. An alternative to comic strips in popular reading were the weekly gossip magazines, illustrated with photographs taken by paparazzi, which recounted the scandalous lives of celebrities in a Rome that had become a substitute Hollywood. The characters in *La Dolce Vita* are bourgeois, and represent a critique and burlesquing of the Italian cultured and ruling class; the structure of the film borrows from the gossip magazines (as well as from Dante's *Inferno*). The emptiness and corruption of the characters' lives are thrown into relief by images of purity and innocence; and yet the cast is endowed with enormous vitality by what Pasolini called Fellini's "indiscriminate and indifferent love." Hitherto Fellini's narratives had been episodic; now they abandon narrative for a fresco of spectacle filmed with a freedom that astonished the public.

1962   *Le tentazionie del dottor Antonio*
        (The Temptation of Doctor Antonio),
        second episode of Boccaccio '70

PRODUCER: Carlo Ponti (Concordia Compagnia Cinematografica and Cineriz, Rome, Francinex and Gray Films, Paris)
SCREENPLAY: Federico Fellini, Tullio Pinelli, Ennio Flaiano, Brunello Rondi, Goffredo Pariser
MUSIC: Nino Rota
DESIGN: Piero Zuffi
EDITOR: Leo Catozzo
LEAD ACTORS: Peppino De Filippo, Anita Ekberg

Fellini had to make this film in color because the other episodes were in color, but it is later, with *Giulietta degli Spiriti,* that he explores its possibilities. Here he responds to outrage at the sexual content of *La Dolce Vita* with a little treatise on the impossibility of repressing sexual desire; a man loses his mask of respectability and literally goes mad as his repressed libido is stimulated by a billboard advertising milk with the image of the sensuous Anita Ekberg. The billboard has speakers and broadcasts a jingle; it is shaped exactly like a CinemaScope screen, and Ekberg moves, climbs down, holds the puny Antonio in a *King Kong* allusion, and eventually strips in exasperation, all of which is commented on for the viewer by a little Eros figure. Fellini is clearly and wittily relating repressed sexual desire to the cinematic experience.

1963   *8½ (Otto e Mezzo)*

PRODUCERS: Angelo Rizzoli, Federico Fellini (Cineriz, Rome, Francinex, Paris)
SCREENPLAY: Federico Fellini, Tullio Pinelli, Ennio Flaiano, Brunello Rondi

PHOTOGRAPHY: Gianni Di Venanzo
MUSIC: Nino Rota
DESIGN: Piero Gherardi
EDITOR: Leo Catozzo
LEAD ACTORS: Marcello Mastrioianni, Anouk Aimée, Sandra Milo, Claudia Cardinale, Rossella Falk

Few films have been as complex as *8½*, yet it avoids obscurity—a phenomenal achievement in a film that is justly regarded as Fellini's masterpiece. Beneath an apparent confusion of reality and fantasy, Fellini weaves a tight and very ordered web of cinematic self-reflexivity, dovetailing accounts of a film the protagonist *cannot* make, the film he *does* make, as well as the film *Fellini* makes. Jungian psychoanalysis provides Fellini with a scheme for relating memories, dreams and fantasies to the unconscious feelings that animate Guido in his search for an acceptance of the apparently conflicting feelings that paralyze him and that, once accepted, constitute his life and his film. The whole operation is acidly belittled by an omnipresent critic. What made this film so influential for other filmmakers is the richness with which autobiography and filmmaking itself are transformed into cinematic spectacle.

1965   *Juliet of the Spirits (Giulietta degli Spiriti)*
PRODUCER: Angelo Rizzoli (Federiz, Rome, Francoriz, Paris)
SCREENPLAY: Federico Fellini, Tullio Pinelli, Ennio Flaiano, Brunello Rondi
PHOTOGRAPHY: Gianni Di Venanzo
MUSIC: Nino Rota
DESIGN: Piero Gherardi
EDITOR: Ruggero Mastroianni
LEAD ACTORS: Giulietta Masina, Mario Pisu, Sandra Milo, Lou Gilbert, Caterina Boratto, Luisa Della Noce, Sylva Koscina, Valentina Cortese

This tender film is a rendering into the female of the same

crisis $8\frac{1}{2}$ represented in the male. The departure of Giulietta's husband precipitates a process of confrontation with her past, her fears and her fantasies, which enables her to achieve strength and independence as an individual. Though a far simpler film, structurally, than $8\frac{1}{2}$, Fellini uses color seriously for the first time and makes remarkable use of caricatural types and dream situations to represent a psychic landscape. This is taken further in *Satyricon*.

1967   *Toby Dammit, third episode of Tre Passi nel Delirio (Spirits of the Dead) (or Histoires extraordinaires/Tales of Mystery)*

PRODUCER: Alberto Grimaldi, Raymond Eger (PEA Cinematografica Rome, Les Films Marceau/Cocinor, Paris)
SCREENPLAY: Federico Fellini, Bernardino Zapponi (from a story by Edgar Allan Poe)
PHOTOGRAPHY: Giuseppe Rotunno
MUSIC: Nino Rota
DESIGN: Piero Tosi
EDITOR: Ruggero Mastroianni
LEAD ACTORS: Terence Stamp, Salvo Randone

Fellini, at a low point in his life, uses the Poe tale "Never Bet the Devil Your Head: A Tale with a Moral" as a pretext for a deeply pessimistic portrayal of artistic sterility and despair, together with a searing denunciation of current Italian cinema. A drunken, washed-out English Shakespearean actor arrives in Rome to act in an absurdly pretentious "Catholic" spaghetti western, and kills himself by driving his Ferrari into an abyss.

1969   *Fellini: A Director's Notebook (Block-notes di un Regista)*

PRODUCER: Peter Goldfarb (NBC, U.S.)
SCREENPLAY: Federico Fellini, Bernardino Zapponi
PHOTOGRAPHY: Pasquale De Santis

MUSIC: Nino Rota
DESIGN: Federico Fellini
EDITOR: Ruggero Mastroianni
LEAD ACTORS: Federico Fellini, Giulietta Masina, Marcello Mastroianni

For a U.S. television documentary Fellini subverts the realism and objectivity of documentary (as he did Zavattini's cinema-journalism in *Un'agenzia matrimoniale*) to reassert his creativity after a failed project, populating modern Rome with ancient Romans, and beginning to shoot *Satyricon*.

1969   *Satyricon (Fellini Satyricon)*
PRODUCER: Alberto Grimaldi (PEA, Rome, Les Productions Artistes Associés, Paris)
SCREENPLAY: Federico Fellini, Bernardino Zapponi (from Petronius)
PHOTOGRAPHY: Giuseppe Rotunno
MUSIC: Nino Rota
DESIGN: Danilo Donati
EDITOR: Ruggero Mastroianni
LEAD ACTORS: Martin Potter, Hiram Keller, Max Born, Mario Romagnoli, Fanfulla, Gordon Mitchell, Alain Cuny, Lucia Bosè, Salvo Randone

Still in the crisis that produced *Toby Dammit*, Fellini used Petronius's fragmentary narrative as the basis for his own creation of a dreamlike representation of the search for psychic wholeness, but this time not autobiographical. In *Satyricon* he tried not so much to re-create a real historical period as to exploit the distance in time from the present, which gave him the freedom to represent objectively the "otherness" of the unconscious. Nevertheless, his portrayal of the spiritual decadence of pre-Christian Rome is often seen as a metaphor for the directionlessness of his own age.

1970   *The Clowns (I Clowns)*

PRODUCERS: Federico Fellini, Ugo Guerra, Elio Scardamaglia, (RIA, Rome, ORFT, Paris, Bavaria Film, Munich)
SCREENPLAY: Federico Fellini, Bernardino Zapponi
PHOTOGRAPHY: Dario Di Palma
MUSIC: Nino Rota
DESIGN: Danilo Donati
EDITOR: Ruggero Mastroianni
LEAD ACTORS: Federico Fellini, Liana Orfei, Anita Ekberg, clowns, the film crew

An immensely subtle and witty television documentary about the institution of the clown, *I Clowns* re-creates childhood memories of circus clowns and superimposes a theory of clowning (a repressive, authoritarian type contrasted with an exuberant, chaotic type) on everyday humanity. A history of clowning (which also parodies historical documentaries) then gives way to a fantasy re-creation of the art form.

1972   *Roma (Fellini's Roma)*

PRODUCER: Turi Vasile (Ultra Film, Rome, Les Productions Artistes Associés, Paris)
SCREENPLAY: Federico Fellini, Bernardino Zapponi
PHOTOGRAPHY: Giuseppe Rotunno
MUSIC: Nino Rota
DESIGN: Danilo Donati
EDITOR: Ruggero Mastroianni
LEAD ACTORS: Peter Gonzales, Fiona Florence, Pia De Doses, Federico Fellini, Gore Vidal, Anna Magnani, Marcello Mastroianni

Any attempt to understand by documentary investigation either ancient or modern Rome (for the male Fellini, the feminine city) ends in an impasse. The way to get to its heart is through memory (childhood lessons on ancient Rome, the re-creation of a thirties music hall or the daunting brothels of the period), through the caricatural exuberance of its inhabitants (a Trastevere festival), or through a fantastic vision of Catholic ritual (an ecclesiastical fashion show). The film ends with an amazingly rapid tourist whip around nighttime Rome in the company of a motorcycle gang of latter-day "Vandals."

1973   *Amarcord*
PRODUCER: Franco Cristaldi (FC Produzione, Rome, PECF, Paris)
SCREENPLAY: Federico Fellini, Tonino Guerra
PHOTOGRAPHY: Giuseppe Rotunno
MUSIC: Nino Rota
DESIGN: Danilo Donati
EDITOR: Ruggero Mastroianni
LEAD ACTORS: Bruno Zanin, Pupella Maggio, Armando Brancia, Ciccio Ingrassia, Magali Noël, Francesco Maselli
The rapid art of the caricaturist enables Fellini to create the entire population and its collective rituals of a provincial town in Romagna at the time of his adolescence. But he has said himself that it is the perpetual adolescence of Italians, ever shirking moral responsibility, incapable of growing out of childish sexual fantasies (in which the Church imprisons them), that constituted Fascism and its ridiculous posturings. *Amarcord* is a gloriously comic film that was the only one after *8½* to receive wide public acceptance.

1976   *Fellini's Casanova*
         (Il Casanova di Federico Fellini)
PRODUCER: Alberto Grimaldi (PEA)
SCREENPLAY: Federico Fellini, Bernardino Zapponi, Andrea Zanzotto (verses), Tonino Guerra (lyrics), Antonio Amurri (lyrics), Carl A. Walken (lyrics), Anthony Burgess (English dialogue), from Giacomo Casanova de Seingart's memoirs
PHOTOGRAPHY: Giuseppe Rotunno

MUSIC: Nino Rota
DESIGN: Danilo Donati, Federico Fellini
EDITOR: Ruggero Mastroianni
LEAD ACTORS: Donald Sutherland, Cicely Browne, Tina Aumont, Margareth Clementi, Olimpia Carlisi

Fellini felt disgust for the "nothingness" of the character he had chosen to depict, and yet he uses Casanova to express the fear and awe of men before the creative mystery of the eternal feminine, sunk in the waters of the lagoon of Venice, or deep in the belly of a whale. His remarkable use of Donald Sutherland as a mechanical copulator winding down with old age fits beautifully with the characteristically studied artificiality of the sets.

1978   *Orchestra Rehearsal (Prova d'Orchestra)*
PRODUCTION: Daimo Cinematografica and RAI, Rome, Albatros Produktion, Munich
SCREENPLAY: Federico Fellini, Brunello Rondi
PHOTOGRAPHY: Giuseppe Rotunno
MUSIC: Nino Rota
DESIGN: Dante Ferretti
EDITOR: Ruggero Mastroianni
LEAD ACTORS: Balduin Bass, David Maushell, Francesco Aluigi, Angelica Hansen

At a moment when Italian society seemed to Fellini to be disintegrating into anarchy and threatened by an authoritarian backlash, he made for television with great speed this comic parable of an orchestra that rebels against its authoritarian conductor and cannot, as a result, make music. A steel demolition ball destroying a wall of the auditorium shocks the players into unison, but soon the conductor is abusing the situation by becoming dictatorial. The implied accusation of political irresponsibility was given a conservative interpretation, and displeased nearly everyone.

1980   *City of Women (La Città delle Donne)*
PRODUCER: Opera Film Produzione, Rome, Gaumont, Paris
SCREENPLAY: Federico Fellini, Bernardino Zapponi, Brunello Rondi
PHOTOGRAPHY: Giuseppe Rotunno
MUSIC: Luis Bacalov
DESIGN: Dante Ferretti
EDITOR: Ruggero Mastroianni
LEAD ACTORS: Marcello Mastroianni, Anna Prucnal, Bernice Stegers, Ettore Manni
Sexuality is one of Fellini's main themes. Because he works almost exclusively within his own mental universe (*Giulietta* is an exception), he creates female figures who embody the fantasies of Italian men of his generation and background (which they have acquired as often as not from the cinema). In *La Città delle Donne* Fellini mocks his male characters' incomprehension of any kind of femininity that is not a projection of their own fantasies and insecurities by having his alter-ego protagonist dream of finding himself at a monstrous feminist convention.

1983   *And the Ship Sails On (E la Nave va)*
PRODUCER: Franco Cristaldi (Vides Produzione and RAI, Rome, Gaumont, Paris)
SCREENPLAY: Federico Fellini, Tonino Guerra, Andrea Zanzotto (opera lyrics)
PHOTOGRAPHY: Giuseppe Rotunno
MUSIC: Gianfranco Plenizio
DESIGN: Dante Ferretti
EDITOR: Ruggero Mastroianni
LEAD ACTORS: Freddie Jones, Barbara Jefford, Janet Suzman, Victor Poletti
The ritualistic, aesthetic and emotional aspects of opera and the way it captures the imagination and heart of the spectator

are used as a metaphor for cinema. These are favorably contrasted with contemporary society's obsession with facts, which inexplicably elude the journalist protagonist of this elegant film in which Fellini pursues his polemic on the shallowness and heartlessness of the modern world.

1985   *Ginger & Fred (Ginger e Fred)*
PRODUCER: Alberto Grimaldi (PEA/RAI, Rome, Revcom Films, Les Films Ariane, FR₃ Films, Paris, Stella Films, Anthea, Munich)
SCREENPLAY: Federico Fellini, Tullio Pinelli, Tonino Guerra
PHOTOGRAPHY: Tonino Delli Colli
MUSIC: Nicola Piovani
DESIGN: Dante Ferretti
EDITOR: Nino Baragli, Ugo De Rossi, Ruggero Mastroianni
LEAD ACTORS: Giulietta Masina, Marcello Mastroianni, Franco Fabrizi
This bitter satire on the parasitical nature of television, which lowers everything human to the level of the salable, recalls with affection Fellini's artistic patrimony in variety theater and cinema. The director sees his world of emotion and imagination being snuffed out by a detested reality that apes his art.

1988   *Intervista*
PRODUCER: Ibrahim Moussa (Aljosho Productions, France, RAI-Uno, Rome)
SCREENPLAY: Federico Fellini, Gianfranco Angelucci
PHOTOGRAPHY: Tonino Delli Colli
MUSIC: Nicola Piovani
DESIGN: Danilo Donati
EDITOR: Nino Baragli
LEAD ACTORS: Sergio Rubini, Paola Liguori, Maurizio Mein, Nadia Ottaviani, Federico Fellini, Marcello Mastroianni, Anita Ekberg, members of the film crew

The film about Fellini's own relationship with Cinecittà, his memories of working there in the past, and his present activity shooting an entirely nonexistent film, uses a wealth of devices to drive home the point that the only reality for Fellini is that of his creative imagination, since everything is shown to be an illusion created by him.

1990   *The Voice of the Moon (La Voce della Luna)*
PRODUCERS: Mario and Vittoria Cecchi Gori (CG Group Tiger Cinematografica/RAI-Uno, Rome, Cinemax, France)
SCREENPLAY: Federico Fellini, Tullio Pinelli, Ermanno Cavazzoni (from his novel *Il Poema dei Lunatici*)
PHOTOGRAPHY: Tonino Delli Colli
MUSIC: Nicola Piovani
DESIGN: Dante Ferretti
EDITOR: Nino Baragli
LEAD ACTORS: Roberto Benigni, Paolo Villaggio, Marisa Tomasi, Nadia Ottaviani, Angelo Orlando
The mad and the simple are the only two people sane enough to hear the whisperings of the soul, which are drowned out by the cacophony of modern life and the mass media. Fellini returns to his provincial homeland and its popular culture (using as actors two of Italy's most popular comics) to record this poetic and pessimistic plea for a quieter world in which true communication might be possible.

Films on Which Fellini Did Some Direction

1942   *Gli Ultimi Tuareg (The Last Tuaregs)/I Cavalleri del Deserto (The Riders of the Desert) (never released, possibly not even completed)*
DIRECTORS: Gino Talamo, Osvaldo Valenti (but it is said that Fellini substituted for the director for some scenes)

PRODUCTION: ACI
SCREENPLAY: Federico Fellini, Tito Silvio Mursino (pseudonym of Vittorio Mussolini), Osvaldo Valenti (from a novel by Emilio Salgari)
LEAD ACTORS: Osvaldo Valenti, Luisa Ferida, Primo Carnera

1946 *Paisà (Paisà, Paisan)*

DIRECTOR: Roberto Rossellini
ASSISTANT DIRECTORS: Federico Fellini, Massimo Mida (Fellini directed a sequence in the Florentine episode)
PRODUCERS: Roberto Rossellini (OFI), Rod Geiger
SCREENPLAY: Sergio Amidei, Klaus Mann, Victor Alfred Hayes, Marcello Pagliero, Roberto Rosselini, Federico Fellini, Annalena Limentani (English dialogue), (Vasco Pratolini uncredited)
PHOTOGRAPHY: Otello Martelli
MUSIC: Renzo Rossellini
EDITOR: Eraldo Da Roma

1951 *Periane Chiuse (Drawn Shutters)*

DIRECTOR: Luigi Comencini (the film was started by Gianni Puccini, and it is said that Fellini stood in before Comencini was brought in to replace Puccini)
PRODUCER: Luigi Rovere
SCREENPLAY: Massimo Mida, Gianni Puccini, Franco Solinas, Sergio Sollima (Tullio Pinelli, Federico Fellini uncredited)
PHOTOGRAPHY: Arturo Gallea
MUSIC: Carlo Rustichelli
DESIGN: Liugi Ricci
EDITOR: Rolando Benedetti
LEAD ACTORS: Massimo Girotti, Eleanora Rossi Drago, Giulietta Masina

Films Scripted by Fellini for Other Directors

1939   *Imputato, Alzatevi! (Defendant, On Your Feet!)*
DIRECTOR: Mario Mattoli
SCREENPLAY: Vittorio Metz, Mario Mattoli, Bel Ami (pseudonym of Anacleto Francini) (Giovanni Guareschi, Marcello Marchesi, Vincenzo Rovi, Vito De Bellis, Benedetto Brancacci, Ugo Chiarelli, Carlo Manzoni, Massimo Simili, Stefano Vanzini [Steno], Federico Fellini uncredited)

Lo vedi come sei?!/Lo vedo come sei . . . (Do You See How You Are?)
DIRECTOR: Mario Mattoli
SCREENPLAY: Vittorio Metz, Steno (pseudonym of Stefano Vanzini), Mario Mattoli (Federico Fellini uncredited)

1940   *Non me lo Dire! (Don't Tell Me!)*
DIRECTOR: Mario Mattoli
SCRIPT: Vittorio Metz, Marcello Marchesi, Steno, Mario Mattoli (Federico Fellini uncredited)

Il Pirata Sono Io! (The Pirate Is Me)
DIRECTOR: Mario Mattoli
SCREENPLAY: Vittorio Metz, Marcello Marchesi, Steno, Mario Mattoli (Federico Fellini uncredited)

1942   *Gli Ultimi Tuareg (The Last Tuaregs)/I Cavalleri del Deserto (The Riders of the Desert) (never released, possibly not even completed)*
DIRECTORS: Gino Talamo, Osvaldo Valenti (but it is said that Fellini substituted for the director for some scenes)
PRODUCTION: ACI
SCREENPLAY: Federico Fellini, Tito Silvio Mursino (pseudonym

of Vittorio Mussolini), Osvaldo Valenti (from a novel by Emilio Salgari)

LEAD ACTORS: Osvaldo Valenti, Luisa Ferida, Primo Carnera

1942   *Avanti c'è Posto (There's Room Up Ahead)*
DIRECTOR: Mario Bonnard
SCREENPLAY: Aldo Fabrizi, Cesare Zavattini, Piero Tellini, Federico Fellini (credited as "Federico")

1942   *Documento Z₃ (Document Z₃)*
DIRECTOR: Alfredo Guarini
SCREENPLAY: Sandro De Feo, Alfredo Guarini, Ercole Patti (Piero Tellini, Federico Fellini uncredited)

1943   *Quarta Pagina (The Fourth Page)*
DIRECTOR: Nicola Manzari
SCREENPLAY: Piero Tellini, Federico Fellini, Edoardo Anton, Ugo Betti, Nicola Manzari, Spiro Manzari, Giuseppe Marotta, Gianni Puccini, Steno, Cesare Zavattini (six episodes, each scripted by a different writer, a seventh episode was cut at the editing stage)

1943   *Campo de'fiori (Campo de'fiori Square)*
DIRECTOR: Mario Bonnard
SCREENPLAY: Aldo Fabrizi, Federico Fellini, Piero Tellini, Mario Bonnard

1943   *L'Ultima Carrozzella (The Last Carriage)*
DIRECTOR: Mario Mattoli
SCREENPLAY: Aldo Fabrizi, Federico Fellini

1943   *Chi'ha Visto? (Who Has Seen Him?)*
          (released in 1945)
DIRECTOR: Goffredo Alessandrini
SCREENPLAY: Federico Fellini, Piero Tellini

1944   *Apparizione (Apparition)*
DIRECTOR: Jean de Limur
SCREENPLAY: Piero Tellini, Lucio De Caro, Giuseppe Amato
(Aldo De Benedetti, Federico Fellini uncredited)

1945   *Tutta la Città Canta (The Whole City Is Singing)*
DIRECTOR: Riccardo Freda
SCREENPLAY: Riccardo Freda, Vittorio Metz, Marcello
Marchesi, Steno (Federico Fellini uncredited)

1945   *Rome, Open City (Roma Città Aperta)*
DIRECTOR: Roberto Rossellini
SCREENPLAY: Piero Tellini, Suso Cecchi D'Amico, Aldo
Fabrizi, Alberto Lattuada, Federico Fellini

1945   *Il Passatore (A Bullet for Stefano)*
DIRECTOR: Alberto Lattuada
SCREENPLAY: Sergio Amidei, Klaus Mann, Victor Alfred
Hayes, Marcello Pagliero, Roberto Rossellini, Federico Fellini,
Annalena Limentani (English dialogue), (Vasco Pratolini
uncredited)

1947   *Il Delitto di Giovanni Episcopo*
       (Flesh Will Surrender)
DIRECTOR: Alberto Lattuada
SCREENPLAY: Piero Tellini, Suso Cecchi D'Amico, Aldo
Fabrizi, Alberto Lattuada, Federico Fellini

1947   *Il Passatore (A Bullet for Stefano)*
DIRECTOR: Duilio Coletti
SCREENPLAY: Tullio Pinelli, Federico Fellini, Duilio Coletti
(Cesare Zavattini, Ugo Betti uncredited)

1948   *Senza Pietà (Without Pity)*
DIRECTOR: Alberto Lattuada
SCREENPLAY: Tullio Pinelli, Alberto Lattuada, Federico Fellini,
Ettore Maria Margadonna, Roberto Rossellini

1948   *Il Miracolo (The Miracle), second part of Amore*
        (The Ways of Love)
DIRECTOR: Roberto Rossellini
PRODUCTION: Tevere Film
SCREENPLAY: Federico Fellini, Tullio Pinelli, Roberto
Rossellini
PHOTOGRAPHY: Aldo Tonti
MUSIC: Renzo Rossellini
EDITOR: Eraldo Da Roma
LEAD ACTORS: Anna Magnani, Federico Fellini

1949   *Il Mulino del Po (The Mill on the River)*
DIRECTOR: Alberto Lattuada
SCREENPLAY: Riccardo Bacchelli, Mario Bonfantini, Luigi
Comencini, Carlo Musso, Sergio Romano, Alberto Lattuada,
Tullio Pinelli, Federico Fellini

1949   *In Nome della Legge (In the Name of the Law)*
DIRECTOR: Pietro Germi
SCREENPLAY: Pietro Germi, Giuseppe Mangione, Mario
Monicelli, Tullio Pinelli, Federico Fellini

1950   *Francesco, Guillare di Dio*
        (The Flowers of Saint Francis)
DIRECTOR: Roberto Rosselini
SCREENPLAY: Roberto Rossellini, Federico Fellini, with the as-
sistance of Father Fêlix Morlion, Father Antonio Lisandrini
(Brunello Rondi uncredited)

1950   *Il Cammino della Speranza*
DIRECTOR: Pietro Germi
SCREENPLAY: Pietro Germi, Tullio Pinelli, Federico Fellini

1951   *La Città si Difende*
DIRECTOR: Pietro Germi
SCREENPLAY: Pietro Germi, Tullio Pinelli, Giuseppe Mangione, Federico Fellini, Luigi Comencini

1951   *Persiane Chuise (Drawn Shutters)*
DIRECTOR: Luigi Comencini
SCREENPLAY: Massimo Mida, Gianni Puccini, Franco Solinas, Sergio Sollima (Tullio Pinelli, Federico Fellini uncredited)

1952   *Europa '51 (Europe '51)*
DIRECTOR: Roberto Rossellini
SCREENPLAY: Sandro De Feo, Roberto Rossellini, Mario Pannunzio, Ivo Perilli, Diego Fabbri, Antonio Pietrangeli, Brunnello Rondi (Federico Fellini uncredited)

1952   *Il Brigante di Tacca del Lupo*
        (The bandit of Tacca del Lupo)
DIRECTOR: Pietro Germi
SCREENPLAY: Tullio Pinelli, Pietro Germi, Fausto Tozzi, Federico Fellini

1958   *Fortunella*
DIRECTOR: Eduardo De Filippo
SCREENPLAY: Federico Fellini, Tullio Pinelli, Ennio Flaiano

1979   *Viaggio con Anita (A Journey with Anita,*
        released in the U.S. as Lovers and Liars)
DIRECTOR: Mario Monicelli
SCREENPLAY: Tullio Pinelli (Federico Fellini uncredited)

Films by Another Director in Which Fellini Appeared as Actor

1970   *Alex in Wonderland*
DIRECTOR: Paul Mazursky
SCREENPLAY: Paul Mazursky, Larry Tucker
LEAD ACTORS: Donald Sutherland, Jeanne Moreau, Ellen Burstyn, Federico Fellini

Television Commercials Directed by Fellini

1984   *Television commercial for Campari Soda*
TITLE: "Oh, che le paesaggio!"
1984   Television commercial for Barilla pasta
1992   Television commercials for the banca di roma
Three commercials of 90 seconds each
LEAD ACTORS: Paolo Villaggio, Fernando Rey, Anna Falchi

(Filmography compiled by Chris Wagstaff, courtesy of *Sight and Sound.*)

Index

Page numbers in italic refer to illustrations
F refers to Federico Fellini